BEGINNING **ROCK GUITAR**

Approved Curriculum

The Complete Rock Guitar Method

Beginning • Intermediate • Mastering

PAUL HOWARD

Alfred, the leader in educational publishing, and the National Guitar Workshop, one of America's finest guitar schools, have joined forces to bring you the best, most progressive educational tools possible. We hope you will enjoy this book and encourage you to look for other fine products from Alfred and the National Guitar Workshop.

Revised Edition

Acquisition, editorial, music typesetting and internal design: Nathaniel Gunod, Workshop Arts
Consulting editors: Link Harnsberger and Ron Manus, Alfred Publishing
Cover photo: Jeff Oshiro • Cover design: Ted Engelbart/Martha Widmann

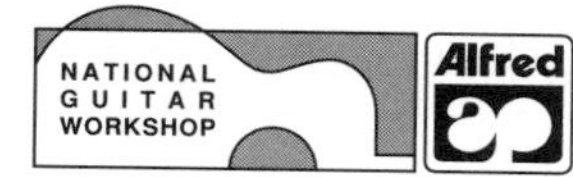

TABLE OF CONTENTS

ABOUT THE AUTHOR

Paul Howard has been a guitar instructor and performer for over twenty years. His experience includes rock, country, folk and jazz on both acoustic and electric guitar. He began private teaching in 1970 and graduated with honors from Central Connecticut State University in 1972. Paul has been a faculty member at the National Guitar Summer Workshop since its inception in 1984. He also operates his own music school in Avon, Connecticut. Paul released two albums with his band, Last Fair Deal, and can be seen playing around New England with the Paul Howard Group. He also tours nationally with the Stacy Phillips/Paul Howard Duo.

DEDICATION

This book is dedicated to all of my students, who, over the years, have taught me much about music and about life. And to my parents, Dorothy and Irving Howard, who encouraged my musical endeavors every step of the way.

ACKNOWLEDGMENTS

Special thanks to: David Smolover, Lou Manzi, Nat Gunod, Miriam Davidson, Ken Parille, Karen Howard and all of my colleagues at the National Guitar Summer Workshop.

INTRODUCTION

This book is the culmination of a lifetime of teaching, observing, studying, listening and playing the guitar. In the following pages you will find the essential information that you need as a beginning rock guitarist.

My experiences working with hundreds of students over the years have influenced the order and content of *Beginning Rock Guitar*. Use this book in a progressive manner—from chapter to chapter. Occasionally, go back to review old material. Everything you have learned since studying it the first time will give you a new perspective. The book can be used with or without an instructor, but the advice and encouragement of a good teacher should not be underestimated. Of course, no book alone can make you a good player. You must practice on a regular basis to begin training your ear, technique, and rhythm.

Often, beginners will overlook their technique. Pay close attention to the technical information presented here and you will learn to play well quickly, with far fewer obstacles.

Good practice is important. Learn all the exercises slowly and carefully, working up speed gradually. Slow and correct is better than fast and sloppy. Expand on the sample licks provided in this book with your own variations. Remember that things can be done many ways on the guitar. When you are ready, spend time learning to solo over the example progressions. They have been chosen to represent as many applications of the material as possible. Tape yourself playing rhythm, maybe with a drum machine, and solo over the playback. Also, checkout some of the play-along practice tapes on the market, such as the *Stand Alone Tracks* series published by The National Guitar Workshop and Alfred.

Rhythm is the single most important element of music. Always work on your "feel" and timing. Try playing drums to work on the rhythmic independence of the different parts of your body. Slapping your knee and tapping your foot works great, too! It is important to work with a metronome or drum machine to improve your sense of rhythm.

Jam with as many people as you can: people who can blow you away, people who can't keep up with you, and especially people from whom you can learn.

There is no substitute for training your ear. It is your ear that will tell you what is—and isn't—working in your playing. Sing. Singing connects your ear to your brain and, in turn, your brain to your fingers. Never forget that.

Learn to read music. It is a language understood by musicians all over the world, regardless of the instrument they play. Tablature is great too, and, combined with standard notation, provides the most complete guitar information.

There is no place for narrow-minded people in the world of music. Seek out advice from other players, friends and idols. Find a good private instructor to unlock new doors for you. There is great music in every style. Listen to it all: rock, jazz, folk, country, classical and all the different categories of each. The legacy of wonderful music left by the musicians of the past is your foundation. Be a team player in a band and bare your soul as a soloist. Above all have fun, develop a positive attitude and let playing music take its rightful place as one of the most rewarding experiences of your life.

CHAPTER 1

Getting Started

This chapter introduces the basic information that is essential for both understanding the guitar and communicating with other musicians. Like any field of endeavor, music has a vocabulary and a system that makes this understanding and communication easier.

Music is a language. Its alphabet is simple. It has only seven letters that are repeated again and again: A - B - C - D - E - F - G - A - B - C etc. Each letter represents a musical sound of a specific *pitch* (highness or lowness). We call these sounds *notes*. Note names recur every eight steps through the alphabet. The distance from a note to the next note with the same name is called an *octave*.

THE GUITAR FINGERBOARD

HALF STEPS AND WHOLE STEPS

Our first order of business is to understand how the guitar fingerboard works and to learn how to find or name all of these notes on the neck. This is easy if we know about *half steps* and *whole steps*.

A half step is the distance from one fret to the next on the guitar. For instance, the distance from the 1st fret to the 2nd is one half step. This is the smallest *interval* (distance between two notes). Two half steps equal one whole step, which is a distance of two frets on the guitar. For instance, the distance from the 1st fret to the 3rd fret is a whole step.

The arrangement of whole steps and half steps in the musical alphabet is as follows:

A B C D E F G A
W H W W H W W

∨ and W = Whole step
‿ and H = Half step

Here is where all of the notes in the musical alphabet —the *natural notes*—are found on the guitar.

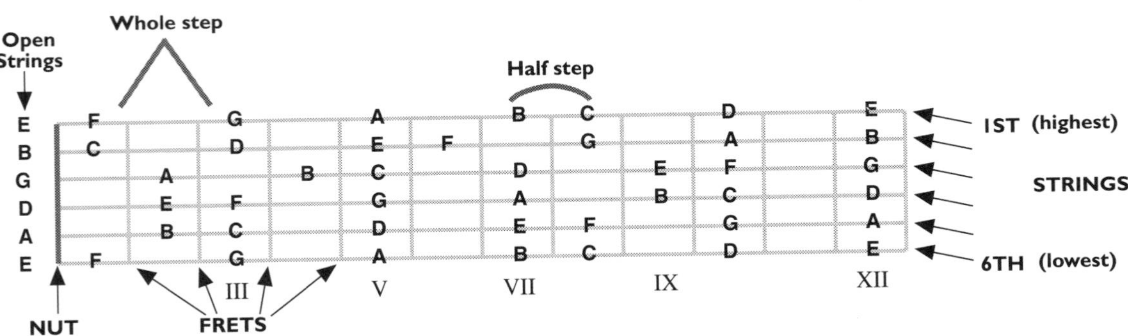

You have probably noticed the blank, unnamed frets on the fingerboard in the diagram on page 6. These are filled with *sharp* and *flat* notes. These are also called *accidentals* or *chromatic tones.* When a sharp ♯ is placed in front of a note, the note is raised one half step (one fret). For example, F♯ is one fret higher than F. When a flat ♭ is placed in front of a note, the note is lowered one half step (one fret). For example, G♭ is one fret lower than G. You will notice that F♯ and G♭ fall on the same fret. Two notes which sound the same (played on the same fret), but are given different letter names, are termed *enharmonic equivalents.* Every sharped or flatted note has an enharmonic equivalent.

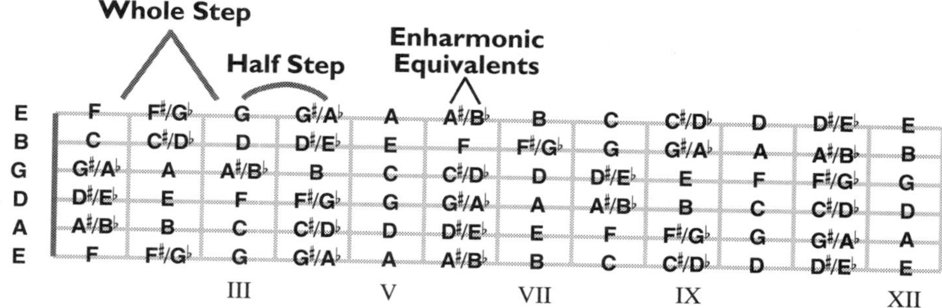

THE CHROMATIC SCALE

The chromatic scale contains all of the natural and chromatic tones. It is composed of half steps. Familiarity with this scale will help you learn the notes on the neck.

A	A♯ or B♭	B	C	C♯ or D♭	D	D♯ or E♭	E	F	F♯ or G♭	G	G♯ or A♭

As you can see, the distance from one note to the next in the scale is always one half step. Also, if you start at any point and count up twelve half steps, you will arrive on the same note name you started with. There are twelve half steps in an octave.

Here is an example of how you can use this information to learn the notes on the guitar:

What note is on the 6th fret of the 6th string?
Refer to the fingerboard chart above. The open 6th string is an E. Find E in the chromatic scale and count up six steps (six frets) starting with F (the note after E). You will arrive at the 6th fret and A♯/B♭. Remember, every chromatic note has two names.

TUNING

There are many ways to get the guitar into standard tuning. Most beginning players tune by comparing the open string to the 5th fret of the next lower string. This works for every string except the 2nd string. To tune the 2nd string, compare it to the 4th fret of the 3rd string.

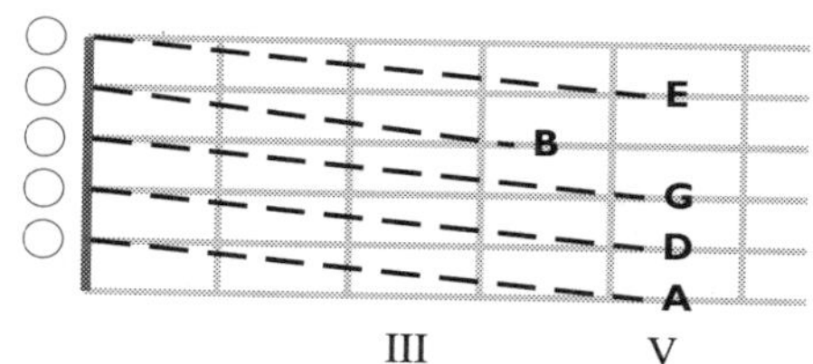

Use a tuning fork or piano to make sure you are tuning to standard concert pitch (A440). Tuning can be greatly simplified by using an electronic tuner, but it is important to train your ear. Any musician must be able to hear when their instrument is out of tune.

MUSIC NOTATION

For purposes of communication, some knowledge of standard musical notation and the most common terminolgy is needed. Nowadays, there are many books and magazines containing educational material and popular rock songs for guitarists. (I wish all of that was available when I was starting out!) If you want to be able to read the arrangements and examples in the books, then this information is for you.

PITCH

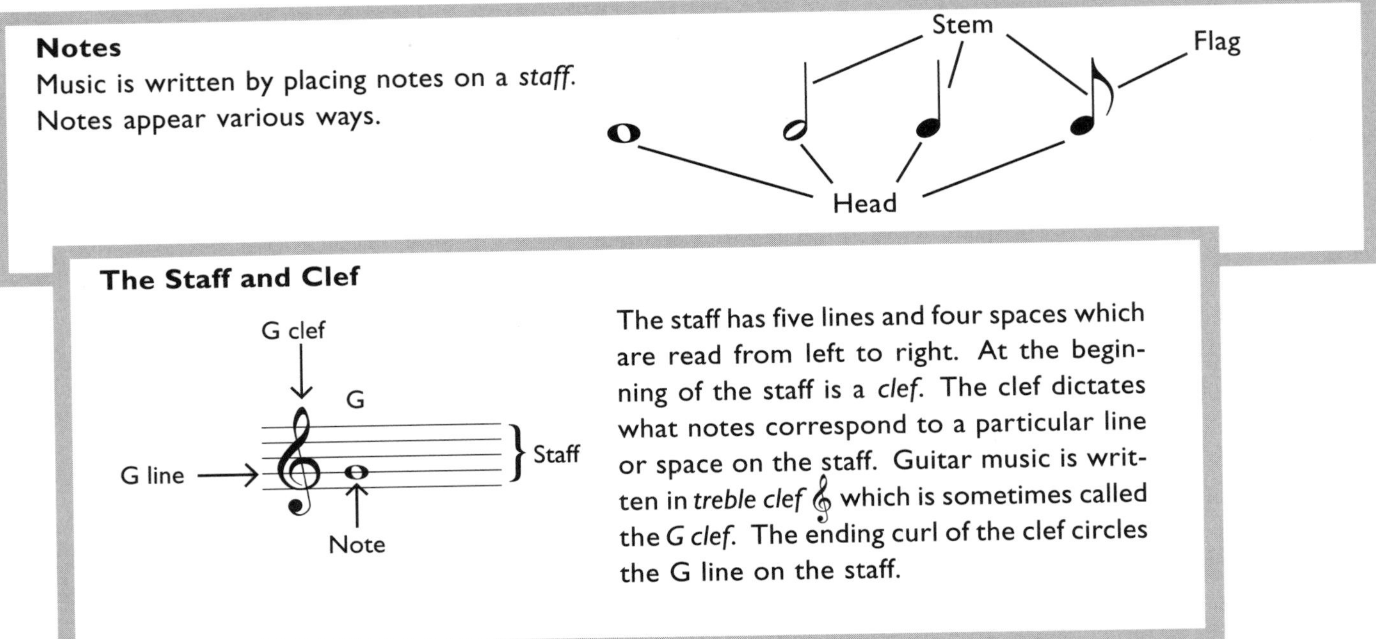

Notes
Music is written by placing notes on a *staff*. Notes appear various ways.

The Staff and Clef

The staff has five lines and four spaces which are read from left to right. At the beginning of the staff is a *clef*. The clef dictates what notes correspond to a particular line or space on the staff. Guitar music is written in *treble clef* 𝄞 which is sometimes called the *G clef*. The ending curl of the clef circles the G line on the staff.

Here are the notes on the staff using the G clef:

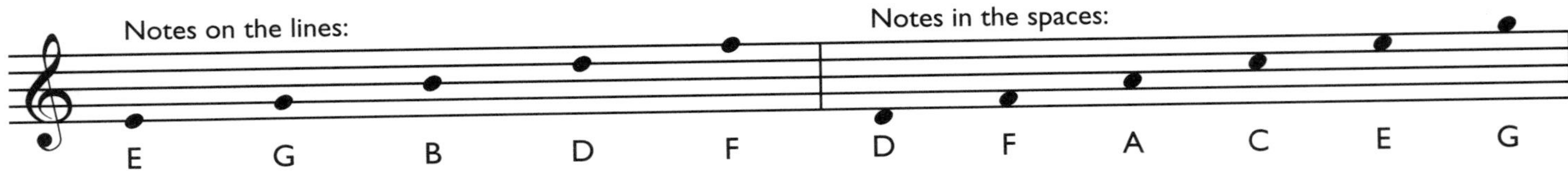

Ledger Lines
The higher a note appears on the staff, the higher it sounds. When a note is too high or too low to be written on the staff, *ledger lines* are used.

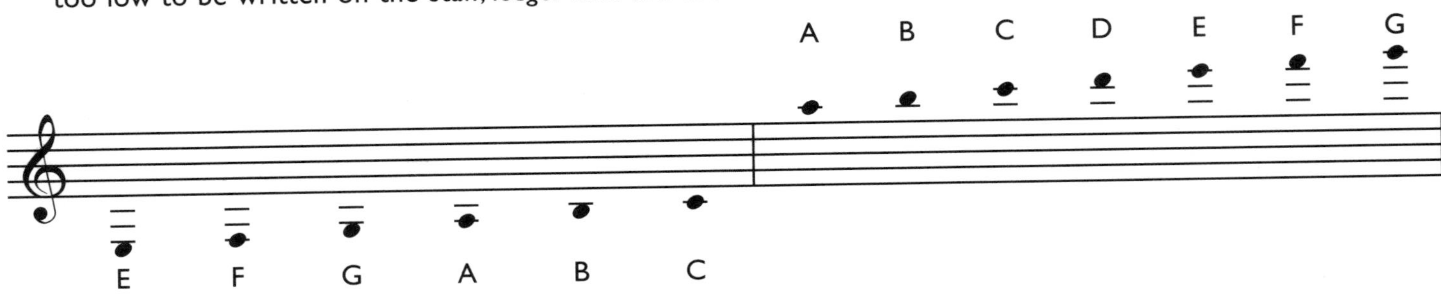

Guitar music actually sounds one octave lower than it is written. We write the music an octave higher than it sounds strictly for reasons of convenience and easy reading.

Measures and Bar Lines

The staff is divided by vertical lines called *bar lines*. The space between two bar lines is called a *measure*. Measures divide music into groups of *beats*. A beat is an equal division of time. Beats are the basic pulse behind music. A *double bar* marks the end of a section or example.

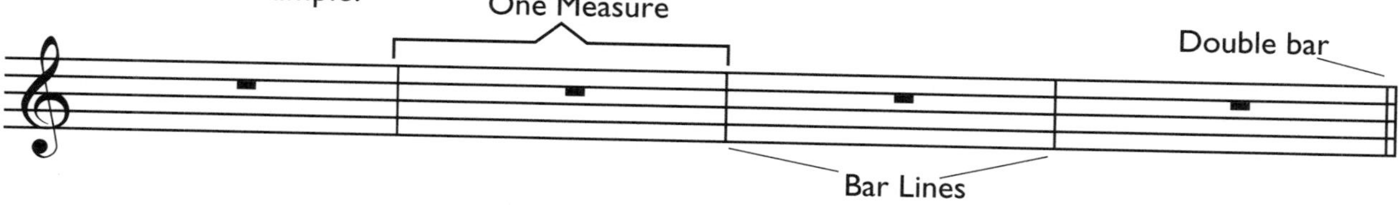

Note Values

As you know, the location of a note relative to the staff tells us its pitch (how high or how low it is). The duration, or value, is indicated by its shape.

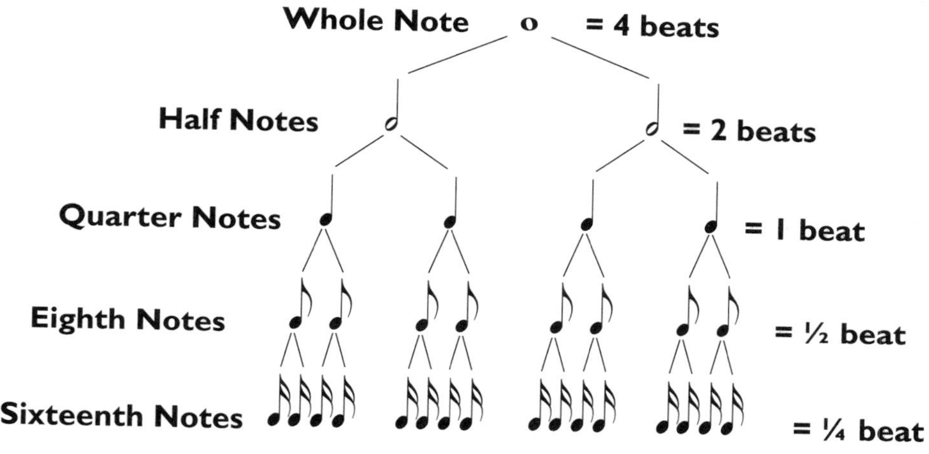

Time Signatures

Every piece of music has numbers at the beginning that tell us how to count time. The top number represents the number of beats per measure. The bottom number represents the type of note receiving one count.

4 ← 4 beats per measure
4 ← Quarter note ♩ = one beat

3 ← 3 beats per measure
4 ← Quarter note ♩ = one beat

6 ← 6 beats per measure
8 ← Eighth note ♪ = one beat

Sometimes a **C** is written in place of $\frac{4}{4}$. This is called *common time*.

Rest Values

Every note value has a corresponding rest. A rest indicates silence. A whole rest indicates four beats of silence, a half rest is two beats of silence, etc.

= Whole rest, 4 beats

= Half rest, 2 beats

= Quarter rest, one beat

= Eighth note, ½ beat

= Sixteenth rest, ¼ beat

Ties

When notes are tied, the second note is not struck. Rather, its value is added to that of the first note. So, a half note tied to a quarter note would equal three beats.

= 3 beats
2 + 1

Notice the numbers under the staff in these examples. They indicate how to count. Both of these examples are in $\frac{4}{4}$ time, so we count four beats in each measure. When there are eighth notes, which are only ½ beat, we count "&" ("and") to show the division of the beats into two parts. When a counting number is in parenthases, a note is being held rather than struck.

Ties are a convenient way to notate notes that begin off the beat (on an "&").

Consecutive eighth notes are *beamed* together. See page 11.

Dots

A dot increases the length of a note by one half of its original value. For instance, a half note equals two beats. Half of its value is one beat (a quarter note). So a dotted half note equals three beats (2 + 1 = 3). A dotted half note is equal to a half note tied to a quarter note.

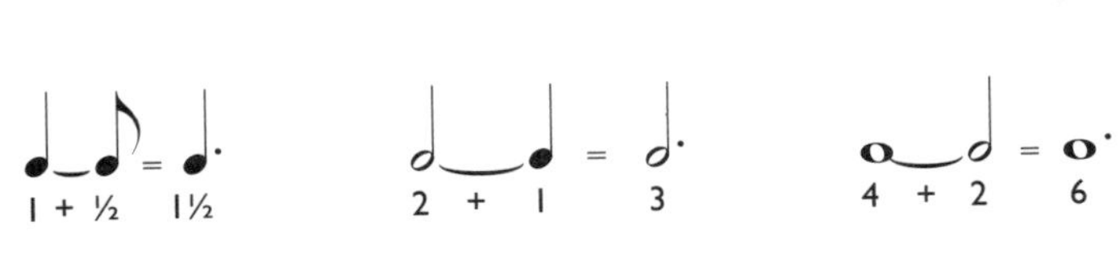

Dotted notes are especially important when the time signature is $\frac{3}{4}$ time, because the longest note value that will fit in a measure is a dotted half note. Also, dotted notes are very important in $\frac{6}{8}$ time, because not only is a dotted half note the longest possible note value, but a dotted quarter note is exactly half of a measure (counted 1 & ah 2 & ah).

Triplets

A triplet is a group of three notes that divides a beat (or beats) into three equal parts.

Beaming

Notes that are less than one beat in duration are often beamed together. Notice the counting numbers: since there are four sixteenth notes in a beat, they are counted "1 e & ah 2 e & ah," etc.

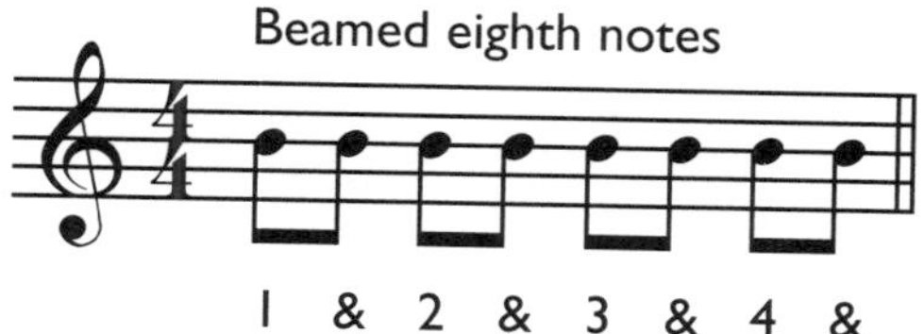

Rhythmic Notation

Rhythmic notation is common in guitar music. It is a system of slash marks with stems and beams that notate specific rhythms without specific pitches. Rhythmic notation is usually used to show a rhythm guitar part.

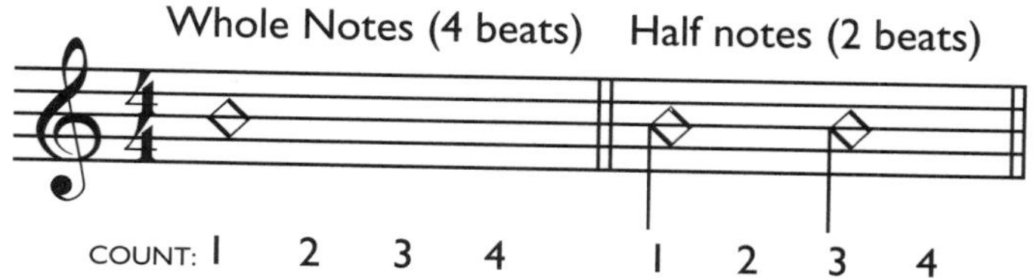

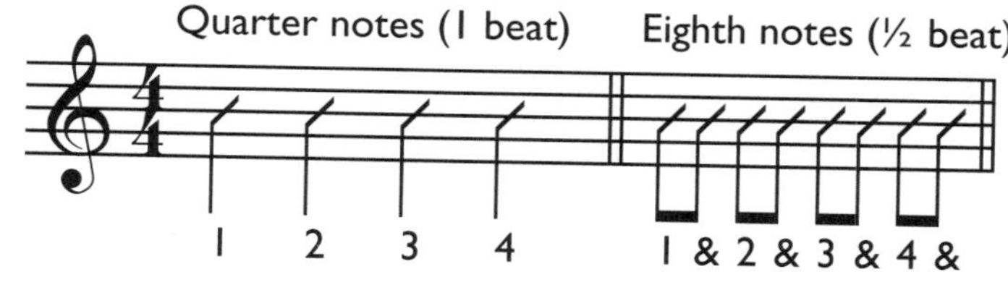

Swing Eighths

Rock music, especially blues oriented rock music, frequently sounds a bit different than notated. The *swing* or *shuffle* rhythm is very commonly played even when regular *straight eighths* are written. *Swing eighths* sound very much like eighth note triplets with a tie between the first two notes in the triplet.

Swing Eighths

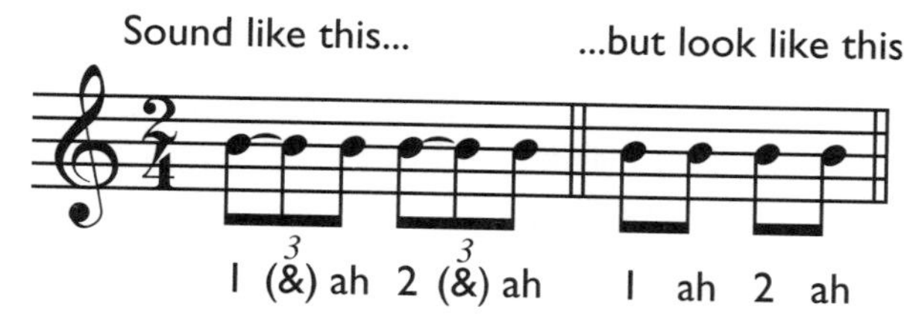

READING TAB, SCALE AND CHORD DIAGRAMS

TAB

Tablature is a system of notation that graphically represents the strings and frets of the guitar fingerboard. Each note is indicated by placing a number, which indicates the fret to play, on the appropriate string.

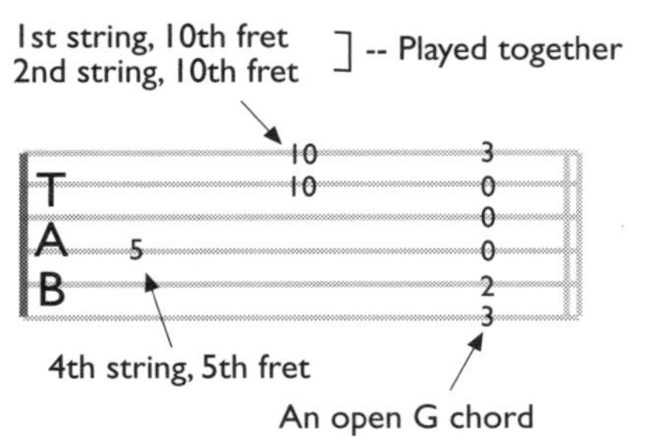

Scale Diagrams

The top line of a scale diagram represents the 1st (highest) string of the guitar, and the bottom line the 6th. The vertical lines represent frets, which are numbered with Roman numerals.

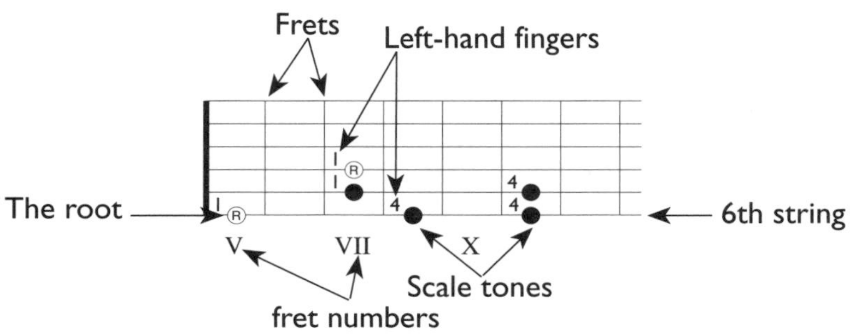

Chord Diagrams

Chord diagrams are similar to scale diagrams, except they are oriented vertically instead of horizontally. Vertical lines represent strings, and horizontal lines represent frets. Roman numerals are used to number the frets.

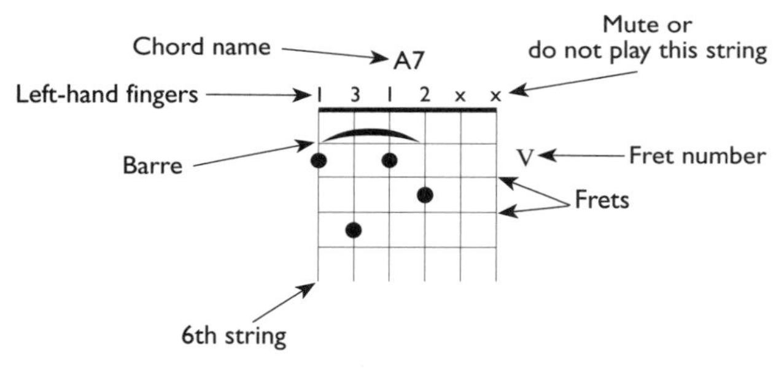

ROMAN NUMERALS

Here is a review of Roman numerals and their Arabic equivalents.

I ..... i 1	IV .. iv .. 4	VII ..... vii . 7	X .... x 10	XIII ... xiii ... 13	XVI ..... xvi 16
II ... ii ... 2	V ... v 5	VIII ... viii 8	XI ...... xi ... 11	XIV ... xiv ... 14	XVII .... xvii ... 17
III .. iii .. 3	VI .. vi .. 6	IX ...... ix ... 9	XII ..... xii . 12	XV .... xv 15	XVIII .. xviii .. 18

SOME TERMS AND SIGNS

Here is a list of the most important terms and signs you will find in this book.

:‖	Repeat. Return to the beginning or the nearest ‖: and play again.
⊓	Pick down. Strike the string by moving your pick down toward the floor.
V	Pick up. Strike the string by moving your pick up toward the ceiling.
H	Half Step. A distance of one fret on the guitar.
W	Whole step. Equals two half steps. A distance of two frets on the guitar.
♭	Flat. Lower the note one half step (one fret).
♯	Sharp. Raise the note one half step (one fret).
♮	Natural. Cancels a sharp or flat.
Root	The note on which a scale or chord is based.
Ⓡ	Root.
PM	Palm mute. See page 27.
>	Accent. To place emphasis on a specific note or chord.
⑤	Circled numbers represent strings. ⑤ indicates the 5th string.
✕	Chuck. Mute the strings with the left hand and strum with the right.
⌒ or ‿	Slur. Used to indicate a hammer-on or a pull-off, and sometimes, a slide.
♩–♩	Slide. Pluck the first note. Slide your left hand finger up or down to the second.

BASIC TECHNIQUE

RIGHT HAND

Most players prefer to hold the pick between the thumb and index finger. Place the pick between the flat pad of the thumb and the left side of the index fingertip. Picking is done in either a downward (towards the floor) or upward (towards the ceiling) motion. Keep the right hand relaxed and hold the pick fairly close to its point. Try a medium gauge pick at first, and then move towards a heavy one as your technique improves.

When playing quicker notes, such as eighth notes, we will usually pick down ⊓ on the number counts (downbeats) and up V on the "&" counts (upbeats). This is called *alternate picking*. With sixteenth notes, pick down on the number and "&" counts and up on the "e" and "ah" counts.

Here are some right hand exerices using the E on the open 1st string.

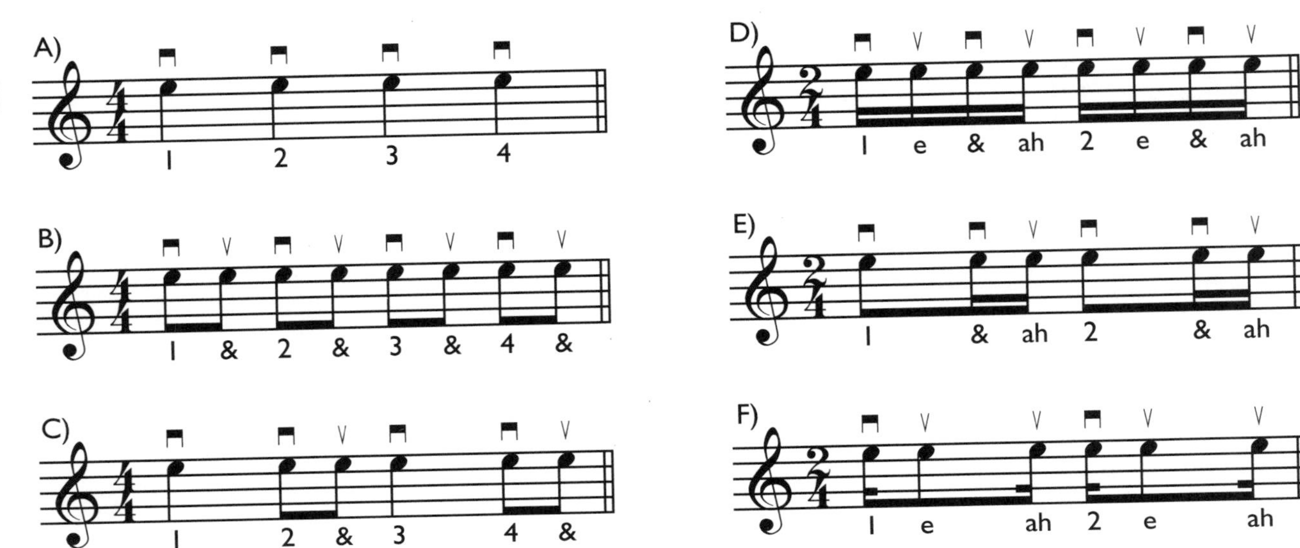

THE LEFT HAND

The proper playing position for the left hand is one which allows you to place all four fingers directly behind the frets. Keep your thumb behind the neck and your wrist low. Do not allow the palm of your left hand to come into contact with the neck. Slightly curl your fingers for maximum leverage and let them do the work, not your hand and arm.

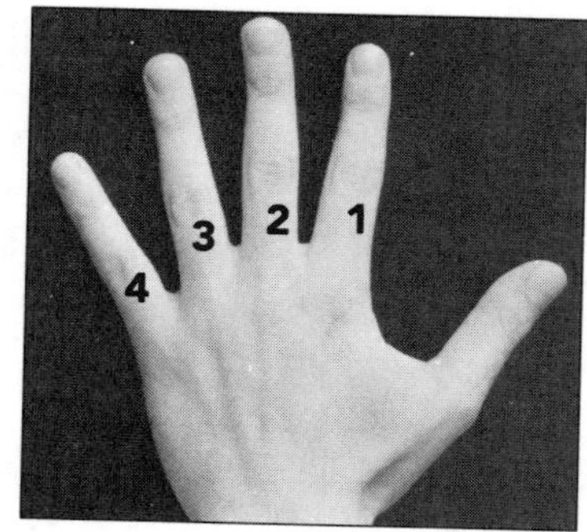

These finger exercies are in the *first position*. In other words, when playing the 1st fret, use your 1st finger, when playing the 2nd fret use your 2nd finger, and so on. Use alternate picking throughout.

Play this sequence twice on each string. Hold your left-hand fingers down until it is absolutley necessary to lift them to play a note on a lower fret.

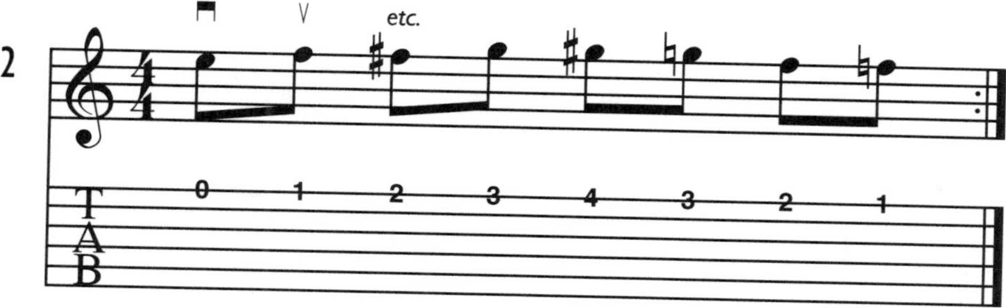

This should also be played twice on each string. The 1st finger should remain down throughout.

This sequence should be played twice on each pair of strings (1st and 2nd, 2nd and 3rd, 3rd and 4th, etc.). Hold down 1 and 3 as 2 and 4 play.

Accidentals remain in force for the entire measure unless they are cancelled by a natural ♮.

Play this sequence up the string for the entire length of the fingerboard and then repeat it on the other five strings. Notice the *slide* lines. To slide, keep your finger on the string as you move to a new fret. We are using the slide technique as a means to *shift* (change positions) up the neck. In Chapter 5 you will learn about slides as an expressive technique.

5

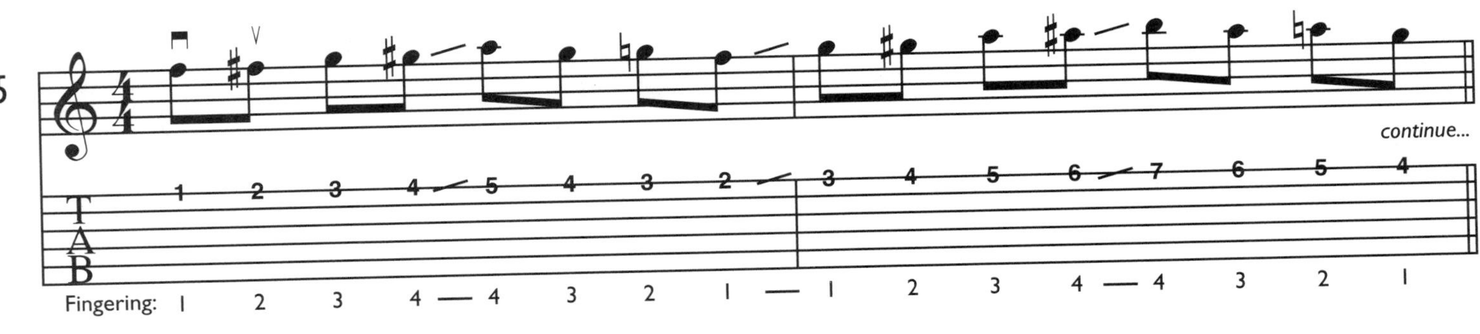

⟋ = slide

After playing this pattern on all of the strings, repeat it one fret higher, and continue up the neck, one fret at a time.

PHOTO • ROBERT KNIGHT

Jimmy Page

CHAPTER 2

Rock Theory

THE MAJOR SCALE

Any discussion of music theory is based on the *major scale* and how other scales and chords relate to it. The major scale is the familiar "do re mi..." scale. A major scale can be sung or played starting on any note. The first note of the scale, the *root* or *tonic*, gives the scale its name. For instance, a major scale starting on the note C is a C Major scale.

A *scale* is a series of notes arranged in a specific pattern of whole and half steps. The letter names always appear in alphabetical order.

A major scale has seven notes. Here is the formula of whole (W) and half steps (H) for the major scale:

W W H W W W H

Below, this formula is applied to a scale beginning on C. Together, these notes comprise the *key* of C Major. Notice that each note in the scale has a numerical name, as well its letter name. For instance, the note D in a C Major scale is the *2nd scale degree*, or "2."

6

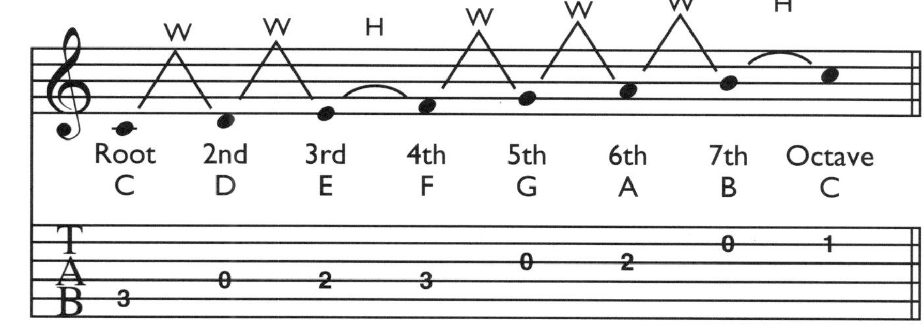

Notice that when the major scale starts on C, the half steps fall naturally between E - F and B - C. No accidentals are required to make the seven notes fit the major scale formula. A major scale built on any root other than C will require either sharps or flats to bring about the correct sequence of whole and half steps.

MAJOR SCALE ON ONE STRING

The major scale pattern is most easily seen on the guitar when played on one string. Start on any note and follow the pattern to build any major scale. Remember: for a half step, go to the next adjacent fret; for whole steps, skip one fret. Name the notes as you play. No letter name can be used more than once (except for the root).

Here is the C Major scale on the 5th string.

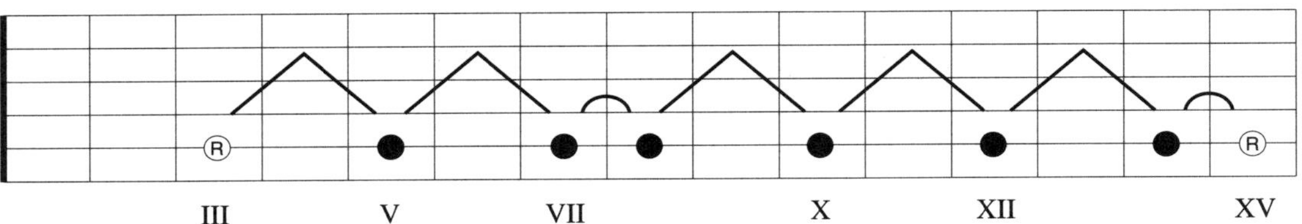

Ⓡ = Root

Remember: This sequence can be played starting on any note on any string.

ONE OCTAVE MAJOR SCALES IN ONE POSITION

A position is a span of four or five adjacent frets. For instance, the 2nd position includes the 2nd, 3rd, 4th, 5th, and sometimes 6th or 1st frets. The 1st finger plays the 2nd fret, the 2nd finger plays the 3rd, etc.

Below is the G Major scale in one position—in this case, 2nd position. Notice that an accidental is needed to make the notes fit the major scale formula. Remember, the notes must be in alphabetical order, and no note name can be repeated. So, the accidental must be F♯, not G♭.

ROOT ON THE 6TH STRING

7

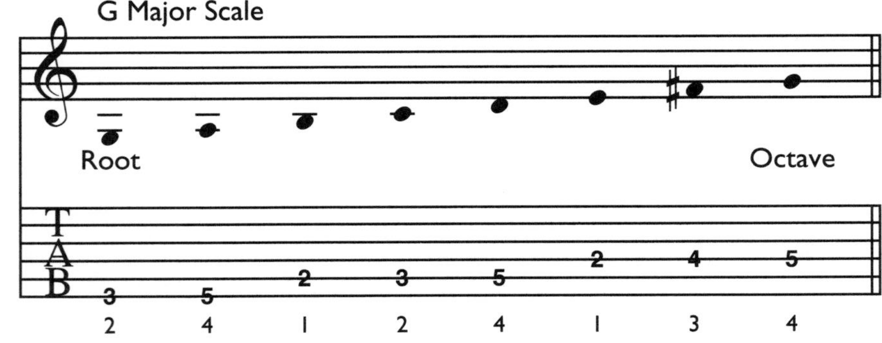

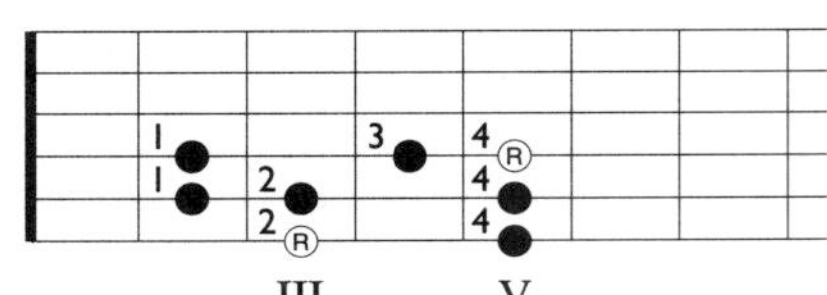

Here are one-octave, one-position major scales in C, F and A.

ROOT ON THE 5TH STRING

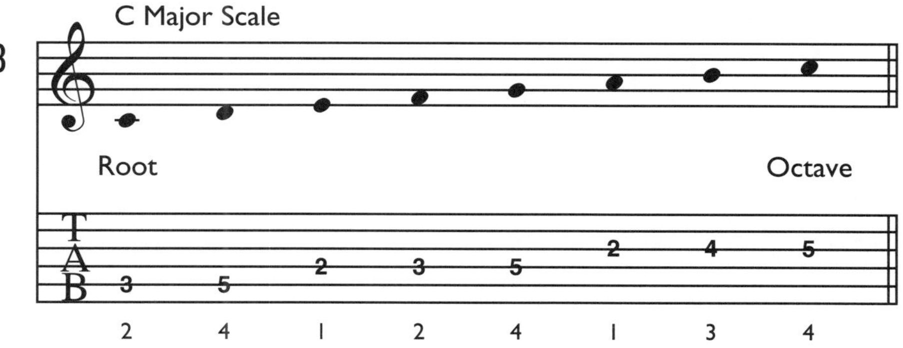

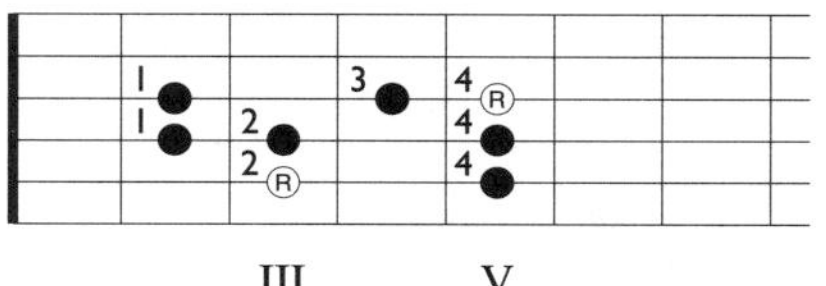

ROOT ON THE 4TH STRING

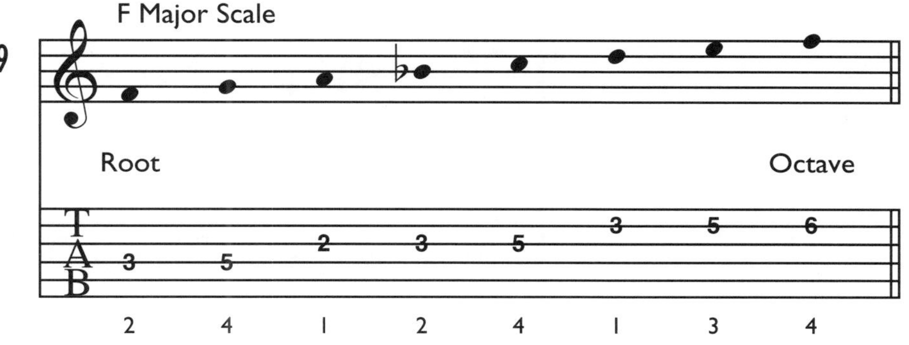

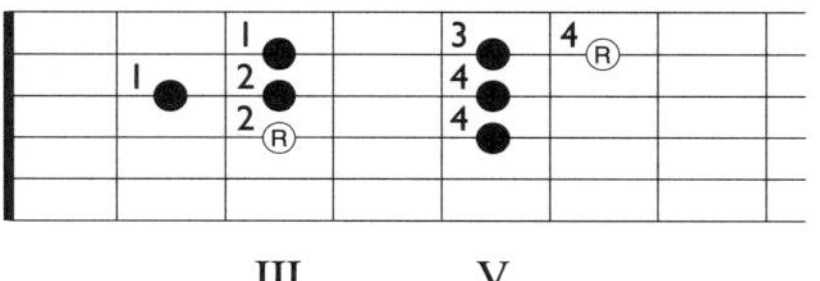

ROOT ON THE 3RD STRING

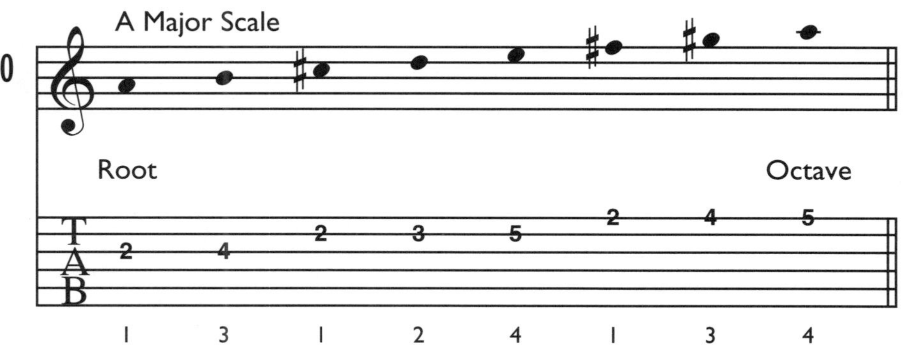

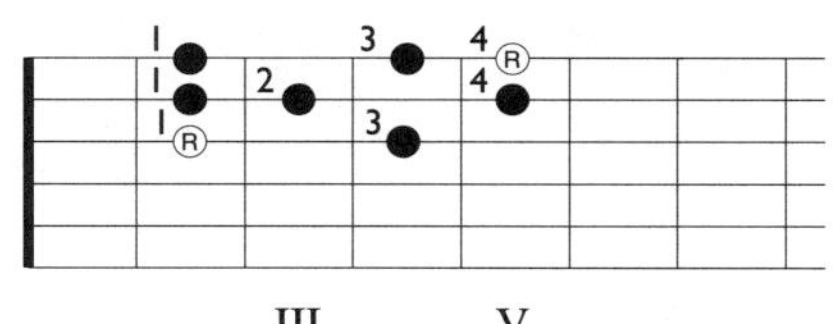

PRACTICING THE MAJOR SCALE

Practicing *melodic patterns* is a great way to learn a new scale. A melodic pattern is melody shape that can be repeated starting on any note.

Pattern #1

Starting on the 2nd fret of the 6th string, continue up the fingerboard.

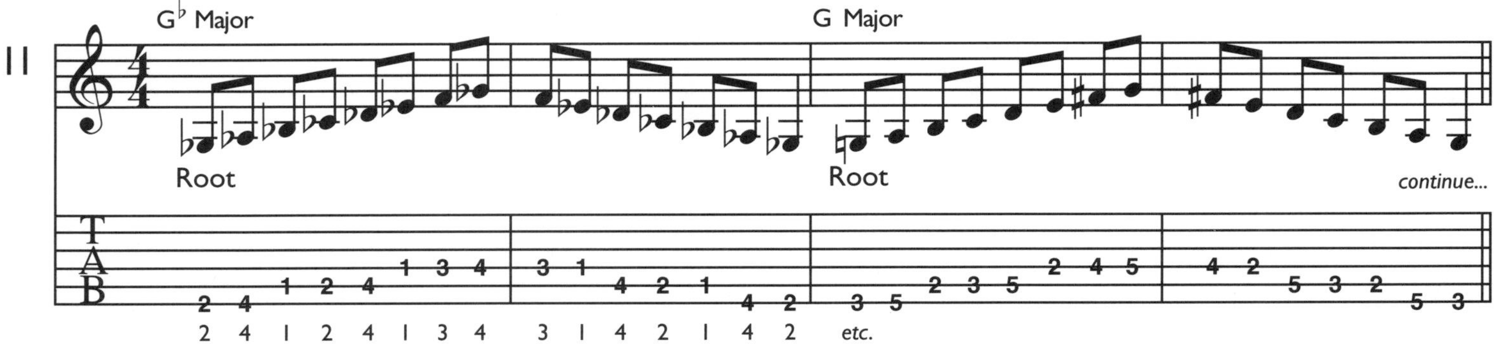

Pattern #2

Starting on the 2nd fret of the 5th string, continue up the fingerboard.

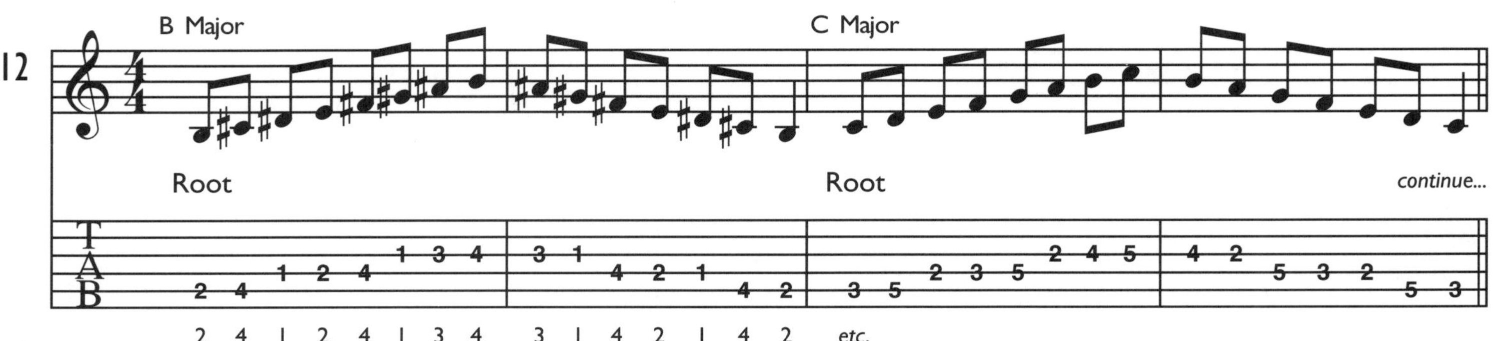

PHOTO • CHUCK PULIN\COURTESY STAR FILES

Duane Allman

Pattern #3

This four-note pattern moves up by step through the C Major scale. The whole pattern can then be continued in C♯, then in D, and so on.

13

Pattern #4

This three-note pattern moves up by step through the C Major scale, and then down again. As with Pattern #3, it can be continued in C♯, then in D, and so on.

14

etc.

continue...

KEY SIGNATURES

The area between the clef and the time signature at the beginning of a piece of music is called the *key signature*. The sharps or flats found in the key signature are derived from the major scale that is the source of all or most of the notes and chords being used. The number of sharps or flats, or their absence, will tell you the key of the piece. In other words, if you see three sharps in the key signature, you know the piece is in the key of A Major, because the A Major scale has three sharps (see page 19, Example 10). One flat means the piece is in F Major (see page 19, Example 9).

RELATIVE MINOR KEYS

For every major key there is a *relative minor key* which is built on the 6th degree of the major scale. For instance, in the key of C, the note A is the 6th degree (C-D-E-F-G-A), so A Minor is the relative minor key of C Major. The A Minor scale would be as follows: A-B-C-D-E-F-G. The distinguishing feature of a minor scale is the smaller interval between the 1st and 3rd degrees (A and C): it is a whole step plus a half step, instead of two whole steps, as in the major scale.

The chart below shows all the flat and sharp key signatures with their corresponding major and minor keys. The key of C Major (and A Minor), has no sharps or flats.

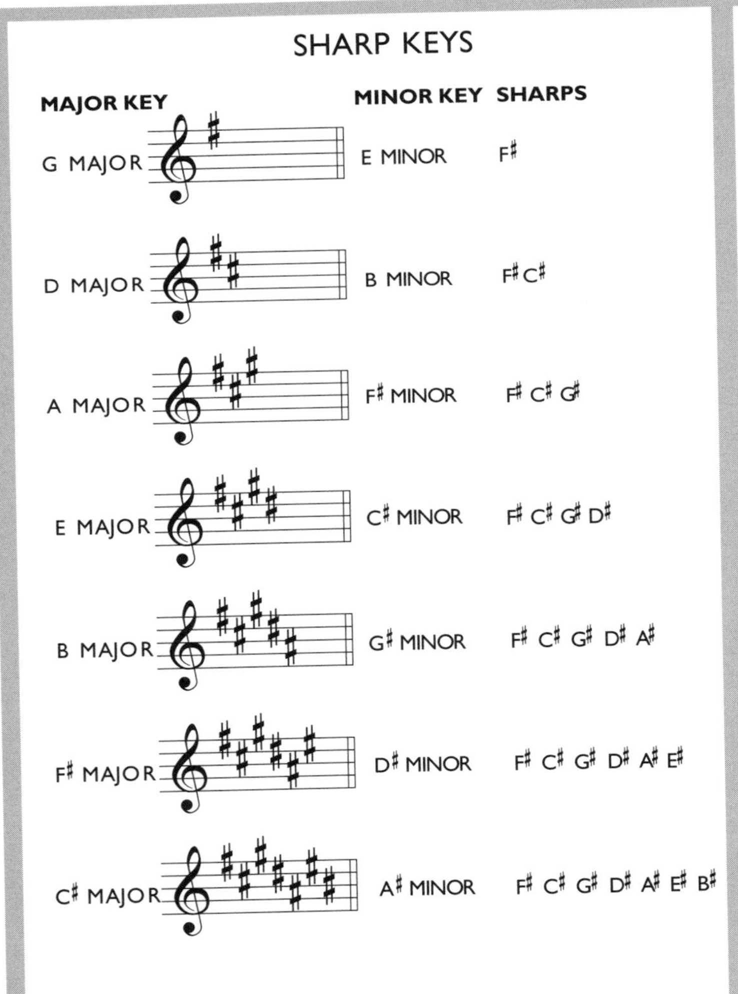

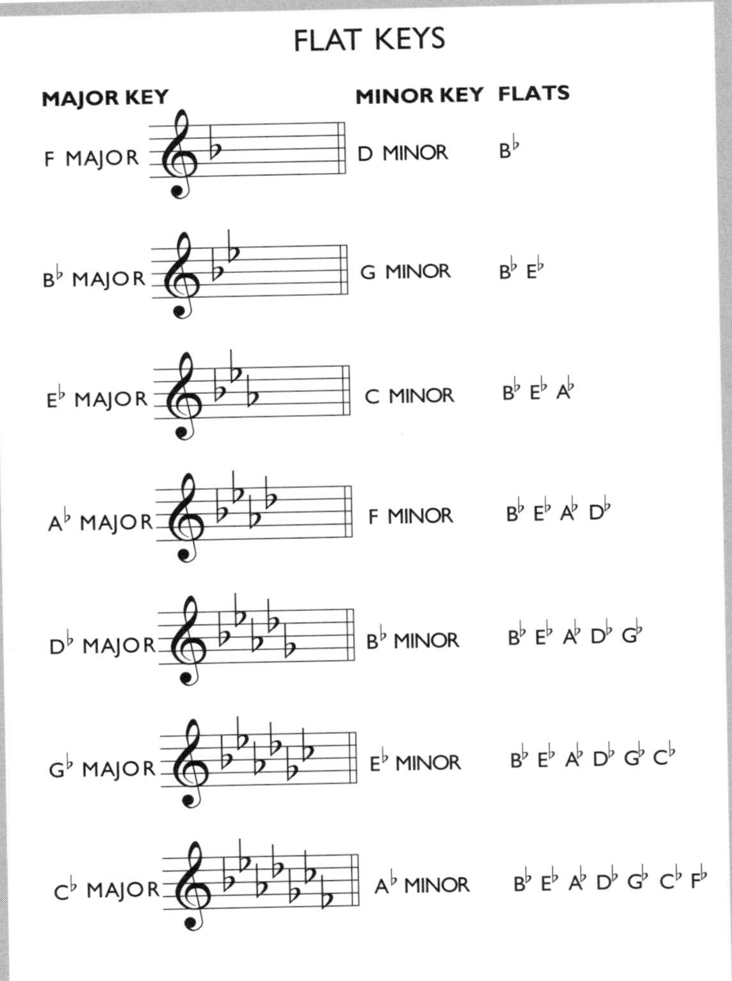

CYCLE OF 5THS

The *cycle of 5ths* is a very useful musical tool that we can use to learn the key signatures.

Here is how to use the cycle:

The key of C is the natural key (no sharps or flats). As you move clockwise through the cycle you will find the names of the keys that have sharps in their key signatures. Each key is a 5th (3½ steps) up from the previous key. The number indicates the number of sharps in that key. To find the notes that are sharped in each key, start with F♯ in the key of G and add a new sharp for each key. The name of the new sharp is always up a 5th from the previous one.

Moving counterclockwise from C, you will find the names of the keys that have flats in their key signatures. Each name is up a 4th from the previous letter. The number indicates the number of flats in that key. To find the notes that are flatted in each key, start with B♭ in the key of F and add a new flat for each key. The name of the new flat is up a 4th from the previous one.

Remember that when counting a 4th or a 5th, include the two names being compared. For instance, C D E F G, C to G is a 5th.

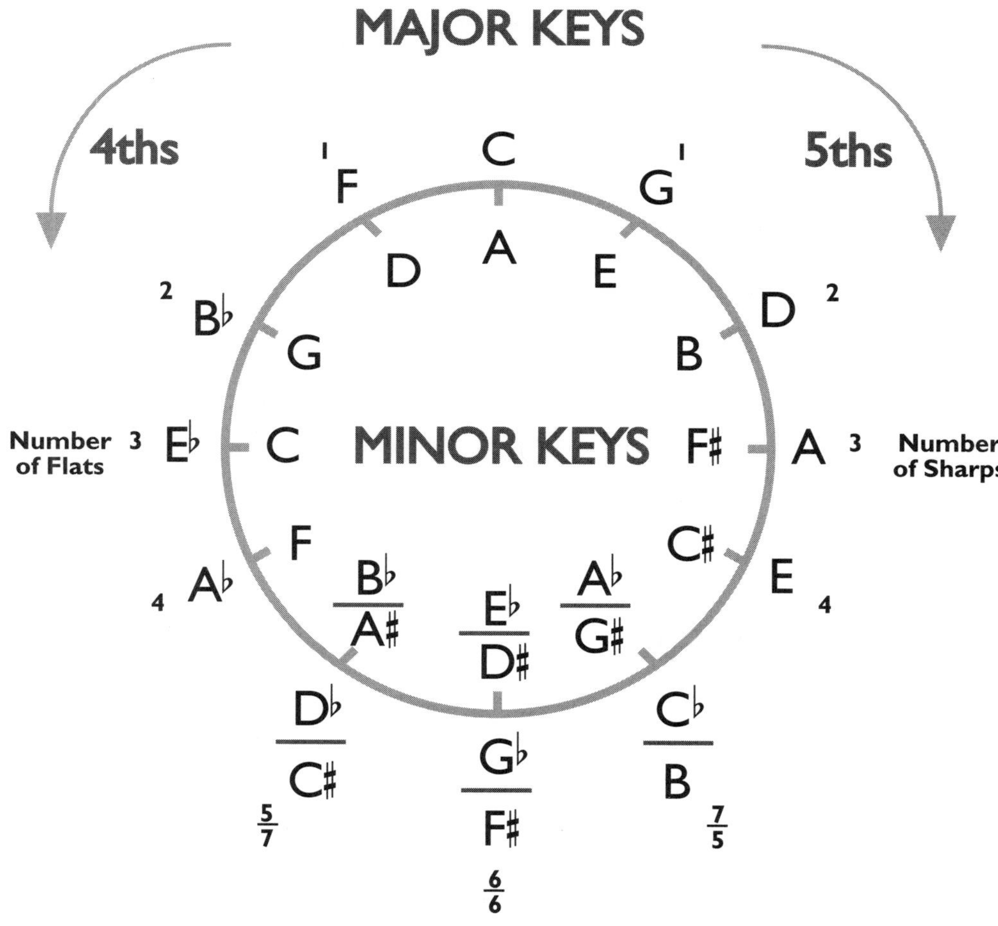

NUMBERING (SPELLING)

Musicians often communicate using *numbering.* In this system, each number refers to a scale degree of the major scale. For instance, in the key of C, the numbers are as follows:

1	2	3	4	5	6	7	1
C	**D**	**E**	**F**	**G**	**A**	**B**	**C**

Any scale or chord can be given a *formula* or *spelling* by comparing the notes involved to a major scale. For instance, if the scale or chord is built on a C root, and contains an E, the E is called 3. If the scale or chord contains an E♭, the E♭ is called ♭3. G would be 5; G♯, ♯5. Here are two samples:

The formula for an A Major scale is

1	2	3	4	5	6	7	8
A	**B**	**C♯**	**D**	**E**	**F♯**	**G♯**	**A**

The formula for an A Minor scale is:

1	2	♭3	4	5	♭6	♭7	8
A	**B**	**C(♮)**	**D**	**E**	**F(♮)**	**G(♮)**	**A**

CHAPTER 3

Power Chords

The *power chord* is one of the most common guitar sounds found in today's rock music. Power chords are used extensively in heavy metal, alternative rock and other rock styles. They are two- or three-note movable forms composed of only roots and 5ths. These forms are *movable* because they have no open strings and the fingered notes can move as a unit up or down the fingerboard. Since there is no 3rd, they are neither major nor minor and can be used in either situation. The root of a power chord is always played by the 1st finger on either the 6th string (Root ⑥), 5th string (Root ⑤) or 4th string (Root ④).

ROOT ⑥

1 3 4 x x x

R 5 R

ROOT ⑤

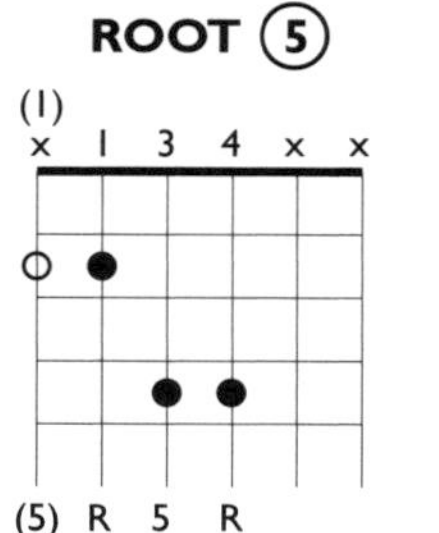

ROOT ④

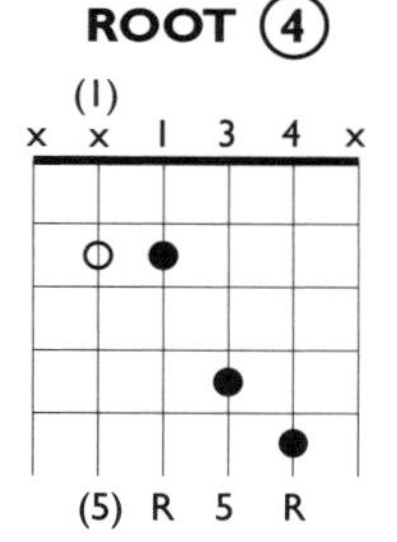

⑥ = A circled number indicates a string
○ = Optional note
x = Mute, or don't strike this string.

A power chord takes its name from the root note being played by the 1st finger. For instance, if the 1st finger is on the note C, the power chord is called C5. They are sometimes called *5th chords* or *no 3rd chords* (C no 3rd).

Here are how power chords are spelled (in C): **1** **5** or **1** **5** **1** (octave)
C **G** **C** **G** **C** (octave)

Root ④ Names for Power Chords

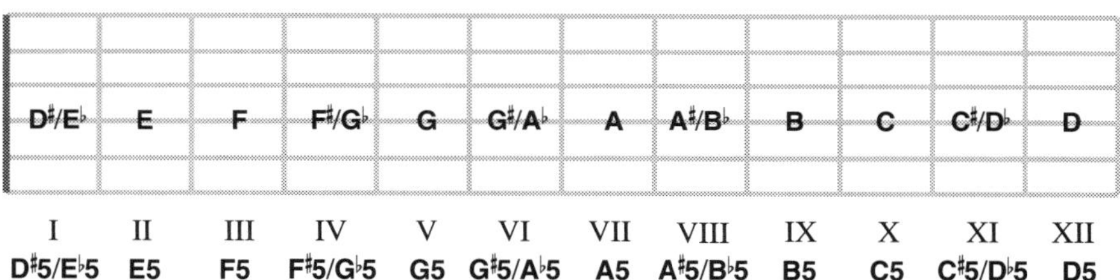

Root ⑤ Names for Power Chords

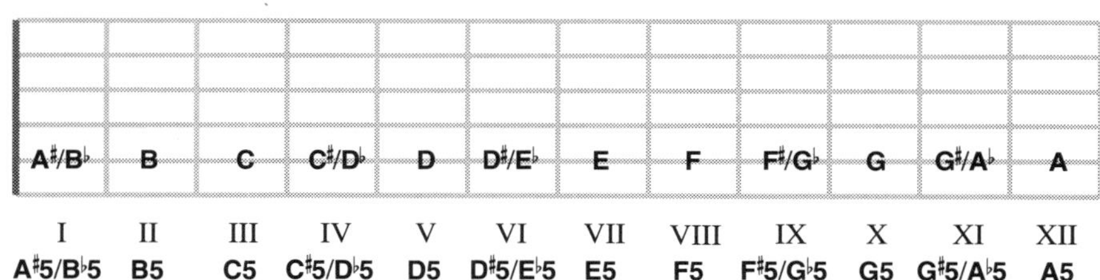

Root ⑥ Names for Power Chords

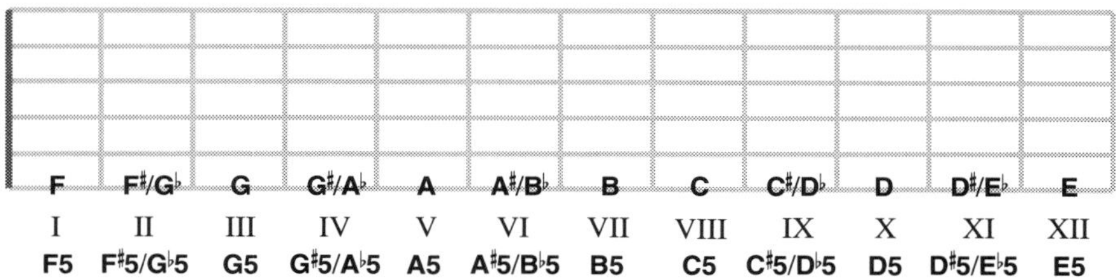

POWER CHORD EXAMPLES

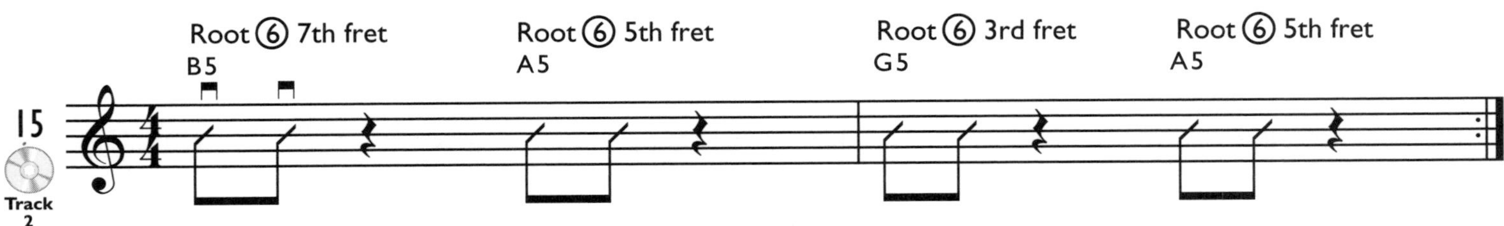

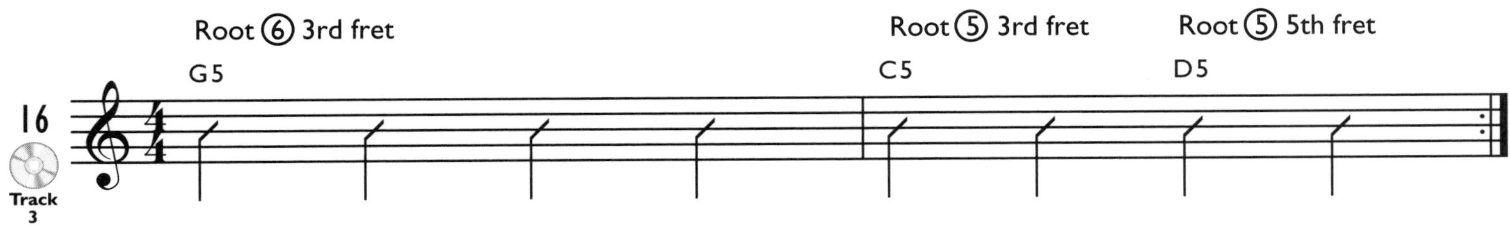

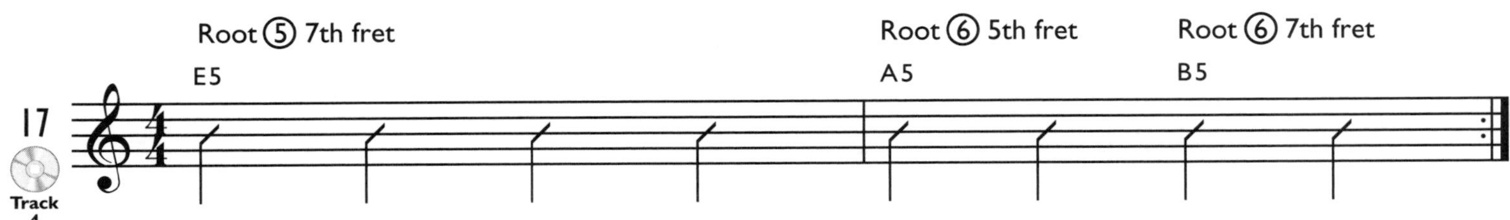

Notice the slide mark ⟋ in Example 18. Strike the strings moving to the new chord, then glide your fingers along the string to the new fret.

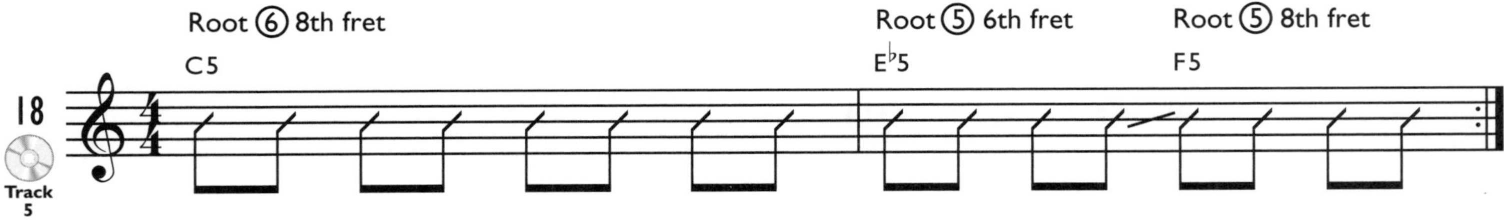

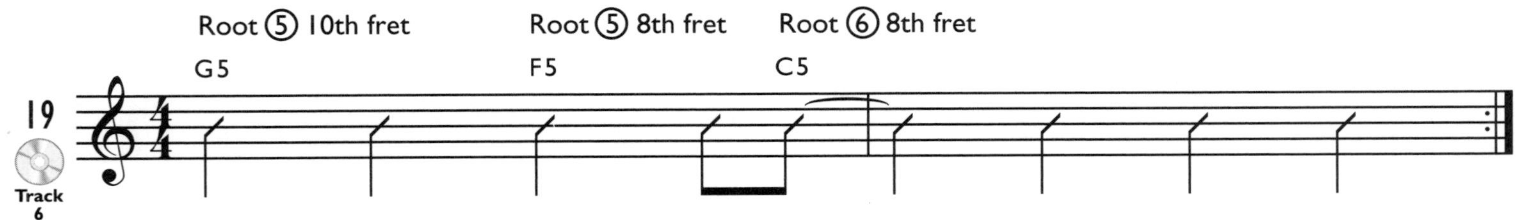

PEDAL TONES AND PALM MUTING

Power chords are often used in conjunction with repeated low notes called *pedal tones* that are usually played on open strings. These notes are frequently muted with the palm of the right hand. Place the palm on the string close to the bridge. This is called *palm muting* (PM).

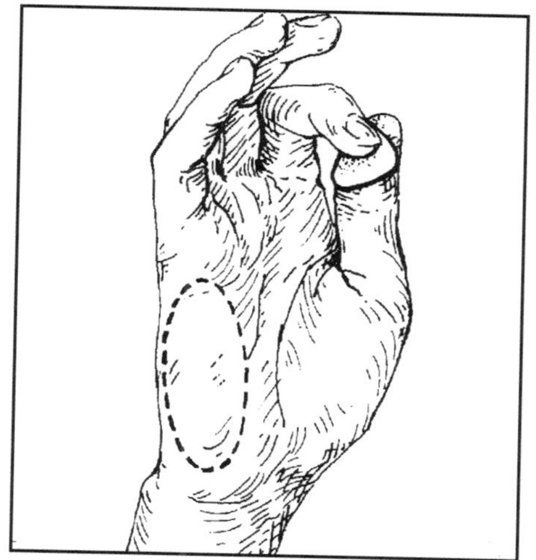
Use this part of your hand to mute.

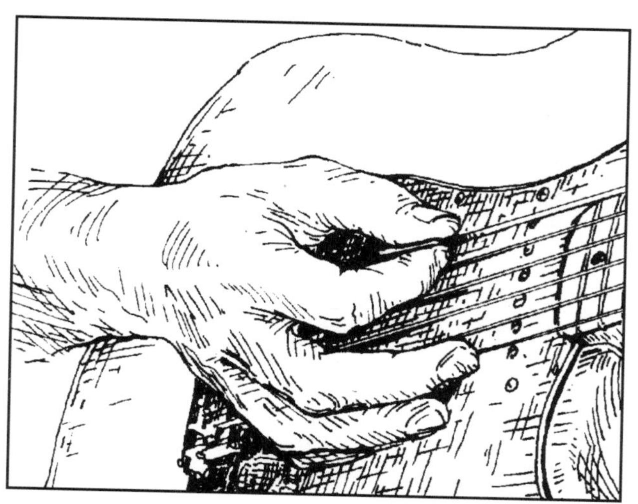
Rest your palm lightly by the bridge.

All Root ⑤ chords

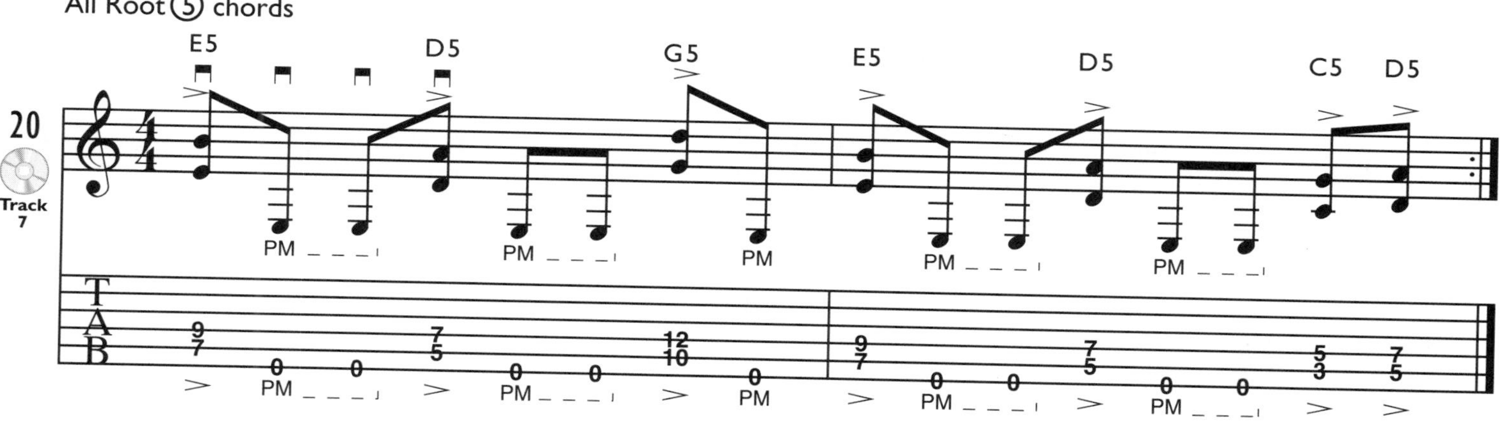

All Root ④ chords

POWER CHORD RIFFS

A *riff* is a catchy, repeated melodic idea that is the basis for a song. Notice the "×" signs in Example 22. These indicate *chucks* or *cuts*: mute the strings with your left hand and strum with your right (see page 52).

In the style of Nirvana

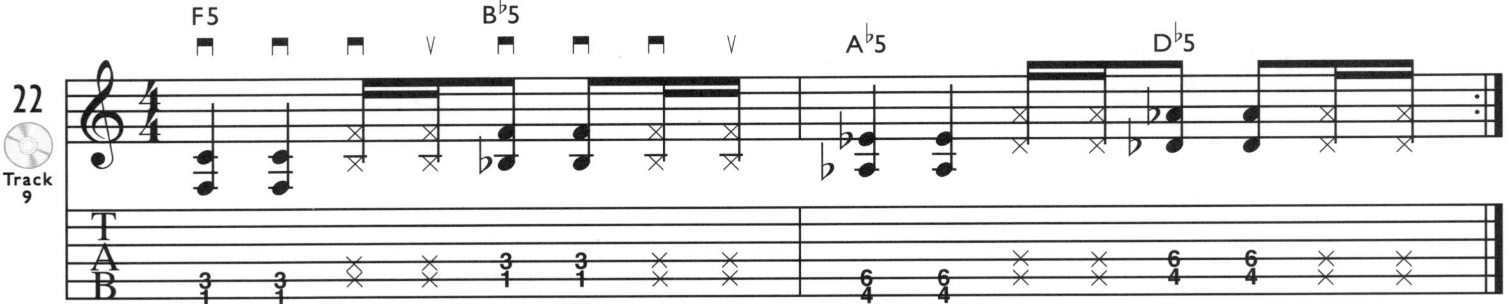

In the style of Green Day

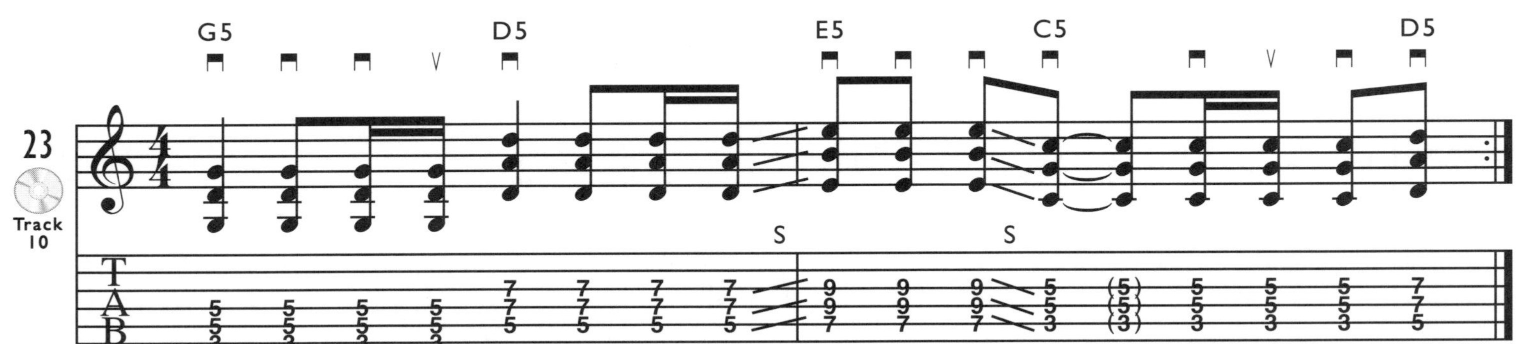

In the style of Led Zeppelin. Note the *slur* marks (‿) in this example. In a slur, only the first note is plucked. See Chapter 5 for more details.

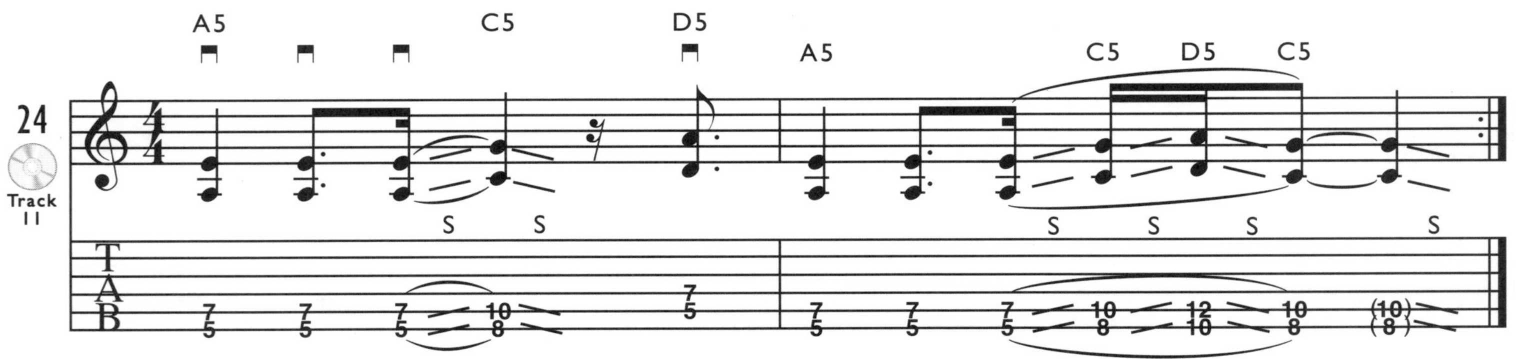

s = slide
╱ = slide up
╲ = slide down

In the style of Black Sabbath

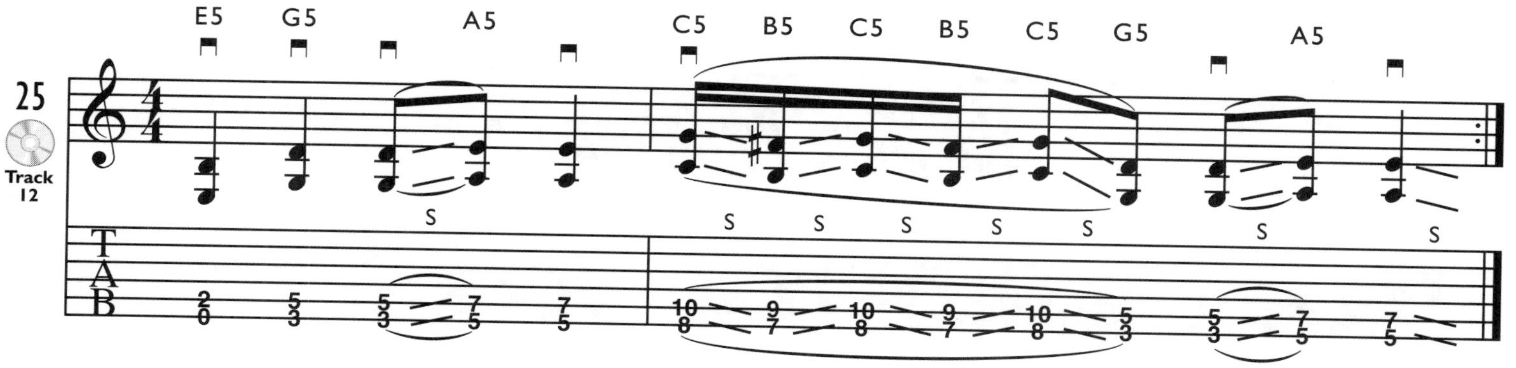

In the style of Cream

In the style of Guns N' Roses

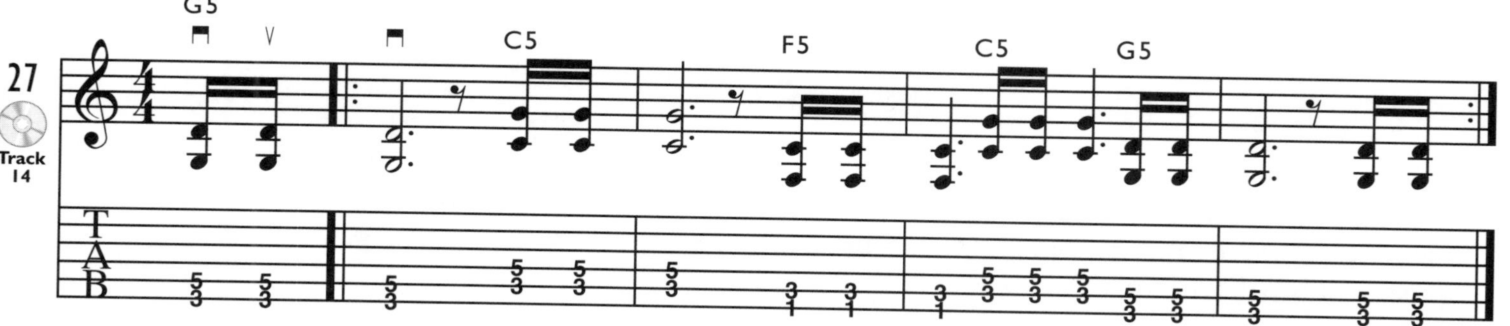

CHAPTER 4

The Minor Pentatonic Scale

IMPROVISATION

Improvisation is the art of spontaneously creating melodies. Usually the improviser uses a vocabulary that includes scales, chords and sounds that are suggested by the key, harmony and style of the music. The improvisor must learn to "speak" expressively by using the appropriate vocabulary to create lines and phrases. See page 32, "Using the Minor Pentatonic Scale" for some important information about phrasing and creating a good solo.

To become a good improviser you must learn the vocabulary for each musical style. Since we are exploring rock guitar, which is basically a blues based style, we will start with the scale that is most often used to improvise in a rock/blues context: *the minor pentatonic scale.*

THE MINOR PENTATONIC FORMULA

Much of rock lead playing is done using the five-note scale called the minor pentatonic scale ("pente" is the Greek word for "five"). The scale is minor because it has a ♭3. These scales can be derived from the seven-note major scale.

MINOR PENTATONIC SCALE FORMULA

1 ♭3 4 5 ♭7

The example below, in the key of E, demonstrates how this formula is used. The five notes of the E Minor Pentatonic scale are selected from the major scale of the same root and then altered according to the formula. Notice that the ♭3 and ♭7 do not have to be flatted notes. If 3 is G♯, then ♭3 is G♮.

E Major Scale	1 E	2 F♯	3 G♯	4 A	5 B	6 C♯	7 D♯
E Minor Pentatonic Scale	1 E		♭3 G♮	4 A	5 B		♭7 D♮

THE E MINOR PENTATONIC SCALE IN OPEN POSITION

28

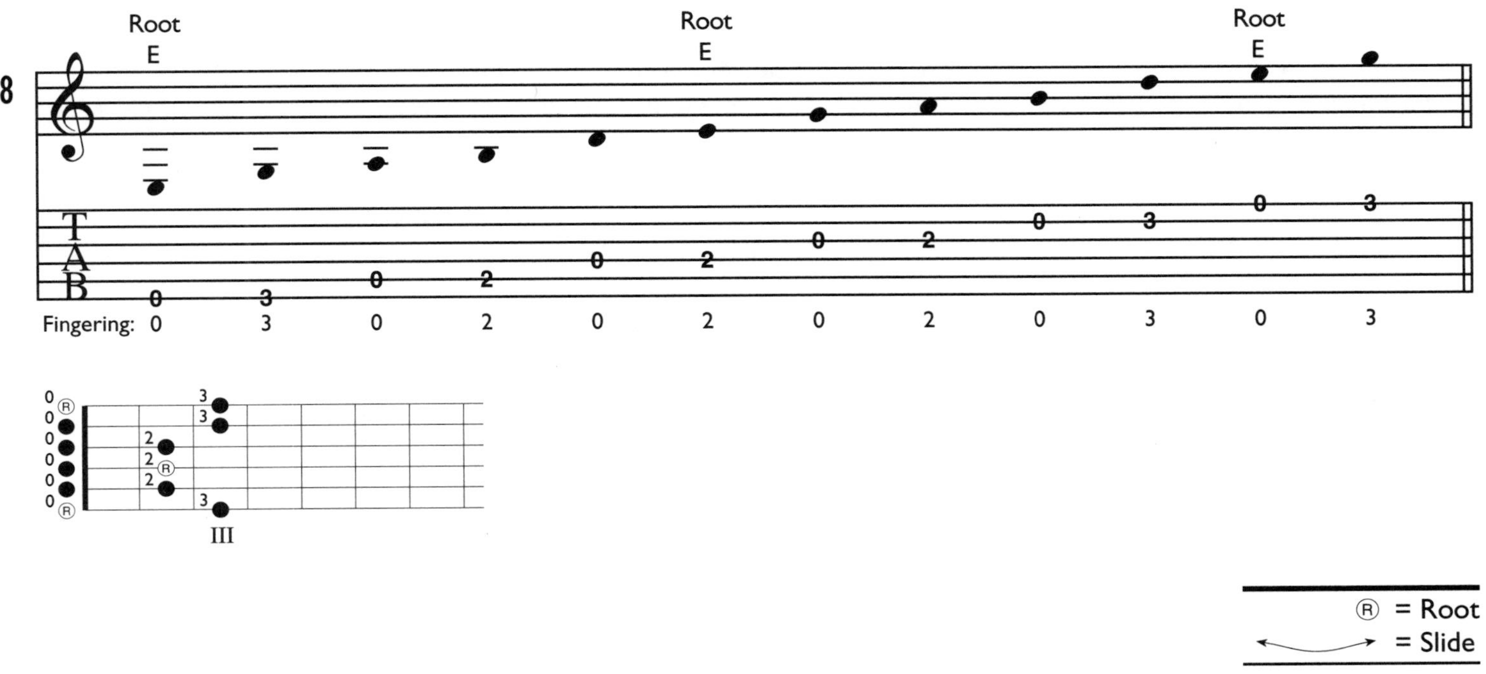

SLIDING E MINOR PENTATONIC

This version of the scale is used for playing E Minor Pentatonic over the entire length of the fingerboard.

29

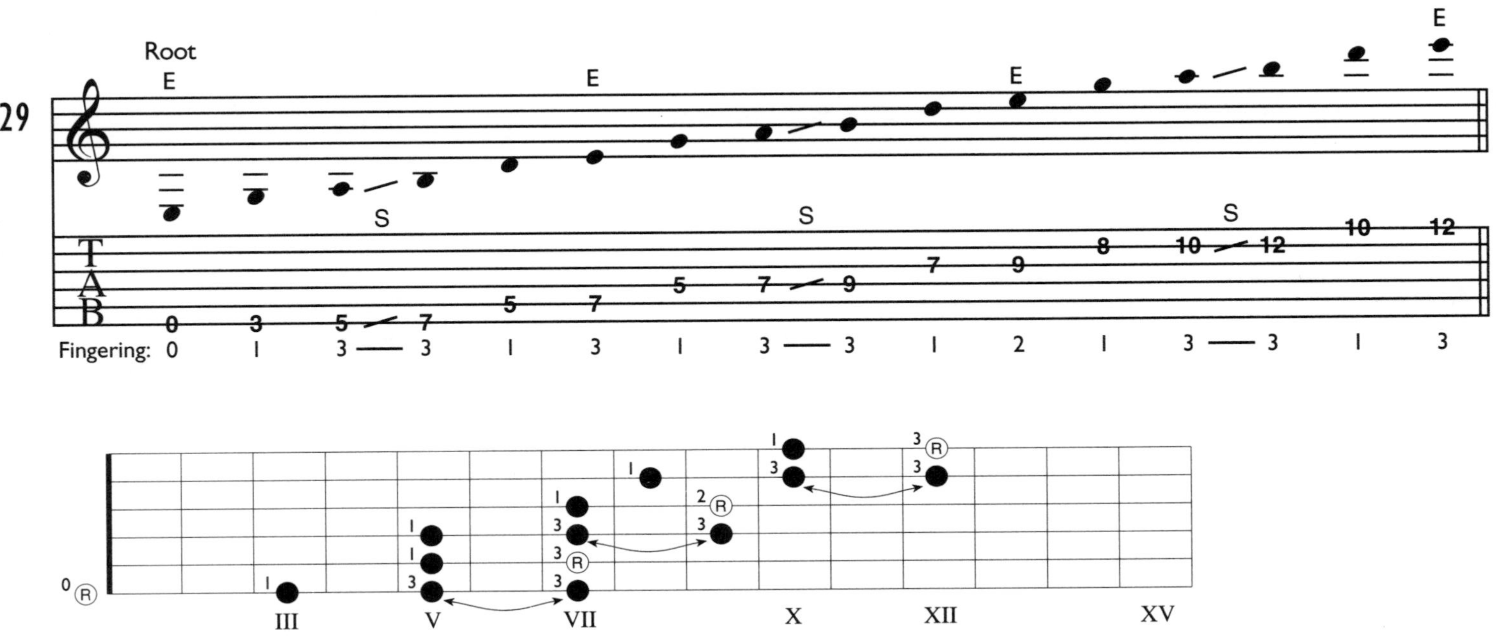

USING THE MINOR PENTATONIC SCALE

As you start to use the scales to improvise, limit yourself to a few notes in one area of the scale. Using these notes, see how much music you can make by varying the rhythm, attack and *timbre* (tone color). At first it is a good idea to be very conscious of where the root notes are in the scale. Try *resolving* (bringing to a close) some of your ideas to these root notes so you can begin to get an idea of *phrasing*. Phrasing refers to grouping notes into ideas. The concept of phrasing is much like the use of sentences when we speak. It helps to increase the understanding for the listener and helps to convey the feeling and meaning of the solo.

Phrasing also contributes to the *shape* and *form* of a solo. The shape of a solo has to do with the rise and fall of notes within the solo. Sometimes a solo may start on low notes and build up to higher notes as the solo progresses. This can help build the solo to an emotional climax. Try to copy this from other solos that you hear. The *form* of the solo has to do with things like single notes leading to *double-stops* (two notes played at once) or chords and other ways of building *dynamics* (volume changes) to get your point across. Your ideas should have a defined length. Endless strings of notes leave the listener unsatisfied. Try developing ideas that have a beginning, a middle and an end.

Remember, improvising is a lot like speaking. Sentences and paragraphs make ideas expressed in words easier to understand. Likewise, phrases, pauses and *dynamic* (volume) changes help the improviser "say" something that will have meaning to the listener.

Getting your feelings across to the listener is very important. Notice that certain groups of notes can make you feel "up" or "down," excited or relaxed. Notice this in solos that you hear and try to copy the feeling—even if you can't copy it note-for-note. Now, stand back and let's wail!

Try playing the minor pentatonic scale to create melodies over the following chord progression. If you do not know how to play these chords, or any other chord in this chapter, see Chapter 6 for more information. Or, use power chords with these root notes.

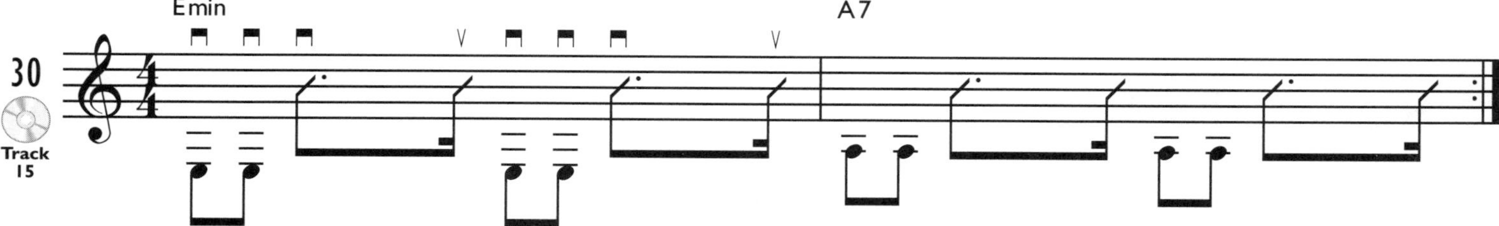

Repetitive chord riffs such as these are relatively easy to improvise over.

MINOR PENTATONIC SCALE FINGERING #1

There are five fingerings of each pentatonic scale. Probably the most commonly used minor pentatonic scale fingering in rock begins with the 1st finger on a root note on the 6th string. We can move the open scale fingering in the key of E that we just learned up an octave by moving the fingering up twelve frets and substituting the 1st finger for the open strings. An E root note is played on the 6th and 1st strings with the 1st finger and on the 4th string with the 3rd finger.

FINGERING #1 IN E

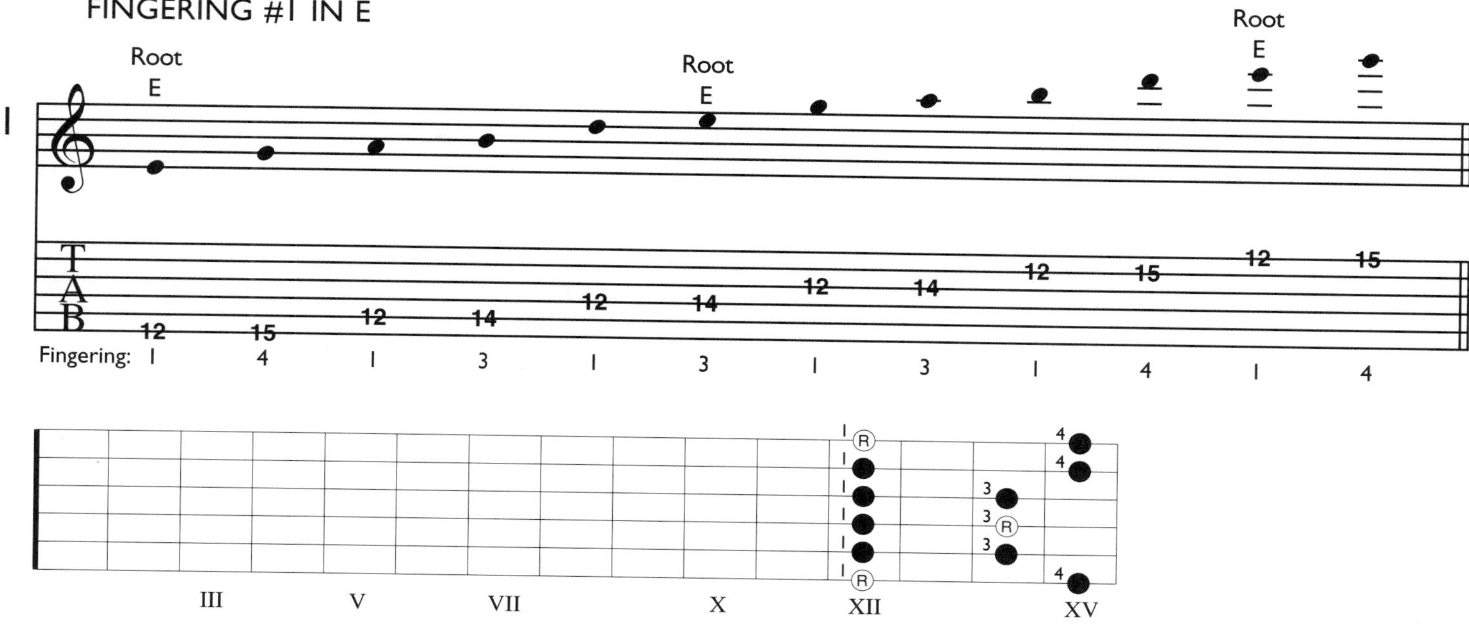

Starting the scale on a different fret (on a different root) allows us to play in a different key. In this case, starting on the 5th fret of the 6th string puts us in the key of A. Remember, *root* means the key note or first note of a scale.

FINGERING #1 IN A

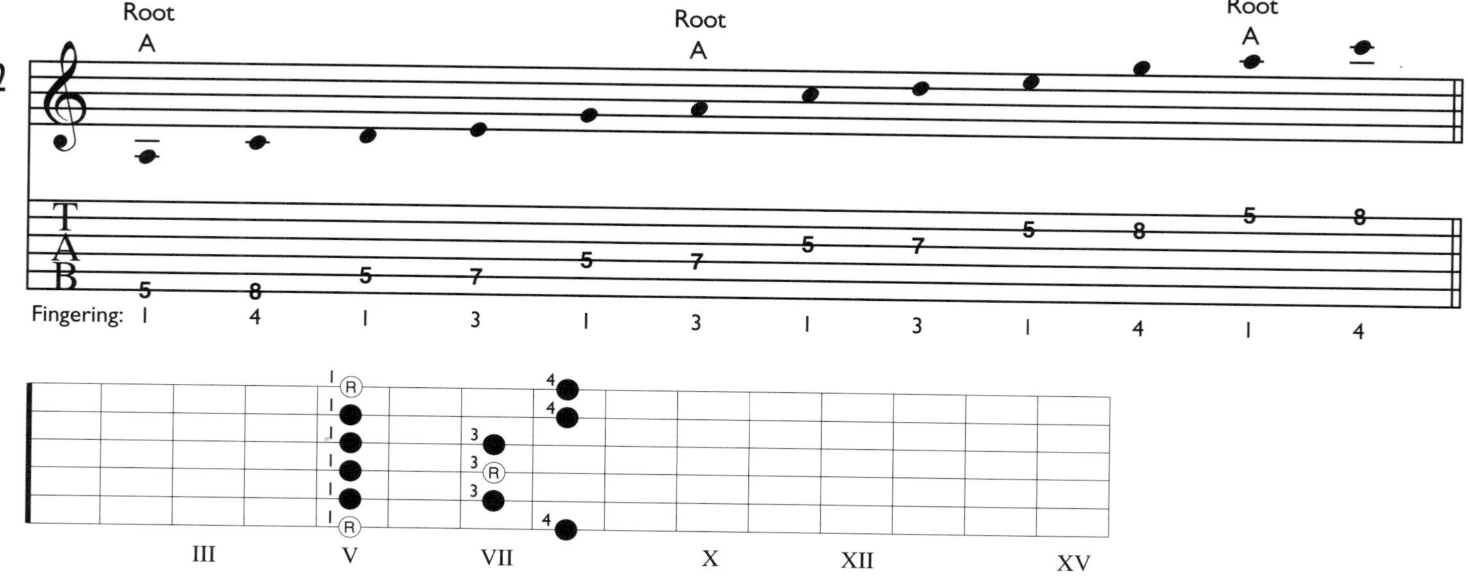

Use the A Minor Pentatonic scale to solo over this chord progression.

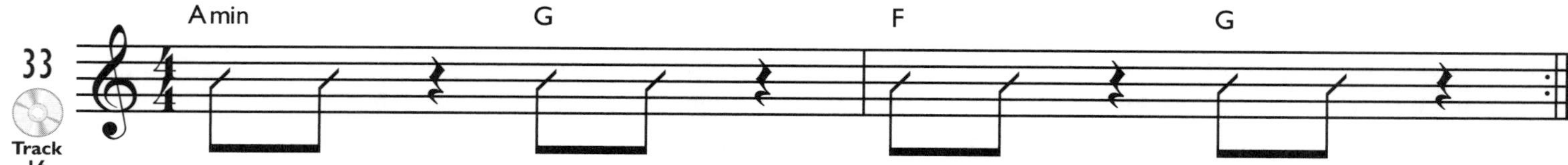

The minor pentatonic scale is often used over chord progressions where the main chord is minor (i). It can also be used over chord progressions in a major key. Practice improvising using the indicated minor pentatonic scales over the following examples. Notice that some of the chord progressions contain major chords. Your minor pentatonic lead creates a characteristic blues sound over those chords.

To learn how to play the chords on this page, see Chapter 6 starting on page 45.

Use the D Minor Pentatonic scale here (the same as fingering as A Minor, but starting on X instead of V).

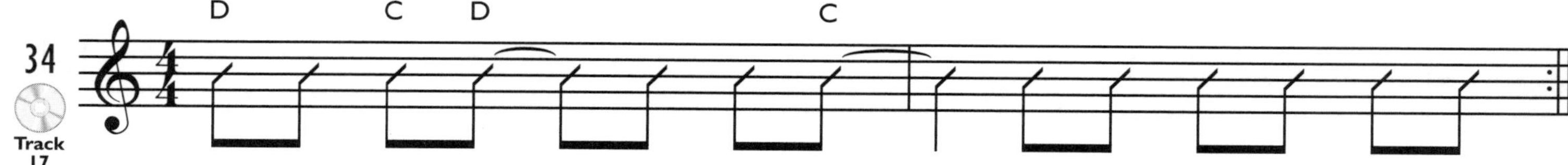

Use the G Minor Pentatonic scale (starting on III) over this twelve-bar blues (see Chapter 8).

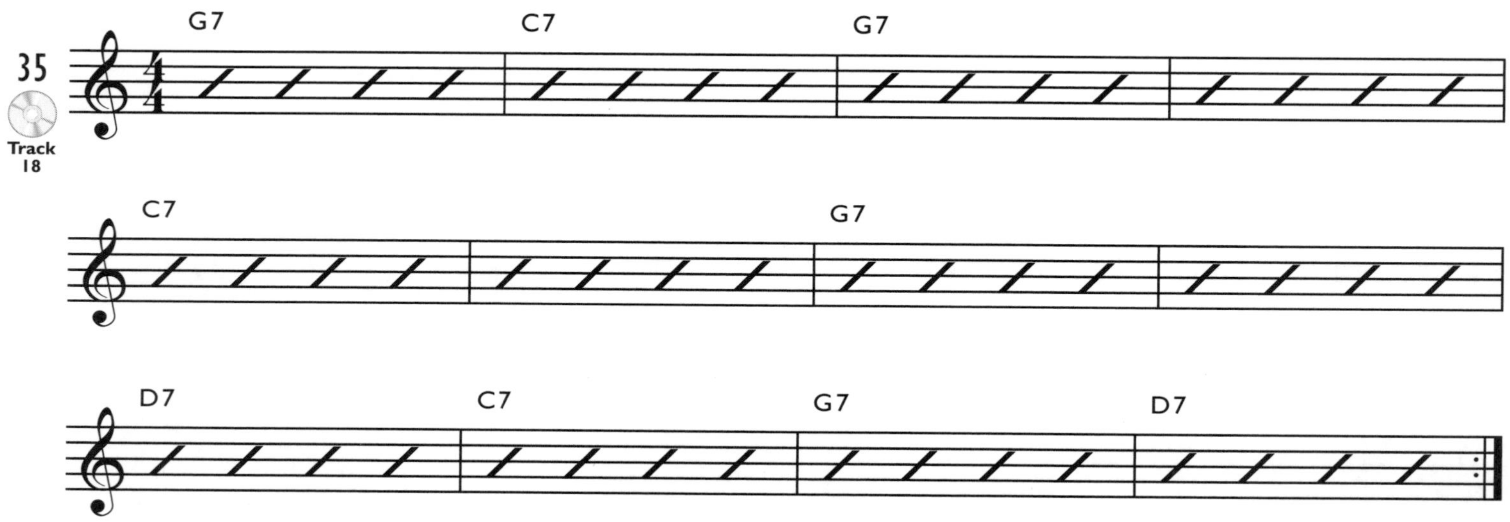

To solo over this progression, use the E Minor Pentatonic scale starting on XII. Or, try the open or sliding E Minor Pentatonic scale fingerings.

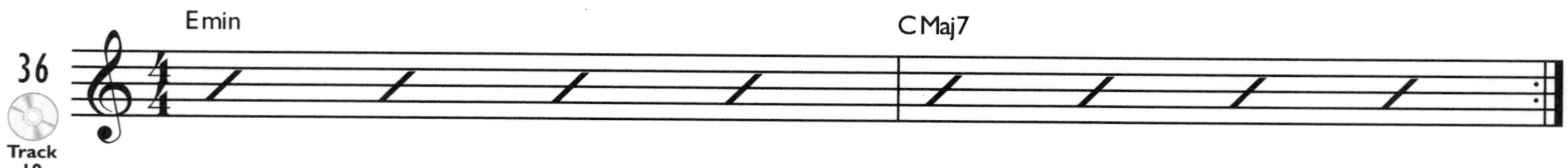

PRACTICING THE MINOR PENTATONIC SCALE

We acquire fluency with any scale by developing a vocabulary of patterns, licks and other building blocks of solos. Begin by playing the scale from bottom to top and vice-versa using alternate picking. Start slowly and gradually increase your speed. Also, practice the following patterns that use the A Minor Pentatonic scale on V. Again, start slowly and speed up as they become more familiar.

CHAPTER 5

Left-Hand Techniques

There are five basic left-hand techniques which are used to add color and variety to single-note playing. Four of these are *slur* techniques. A slur is a *legato* (smooth) change in pitch which is produced solely with the left hand—there is no right-hand attack. The four slur techniques are: *hammer-ons*, *pull-offs*, *slides* and *bends*. A fifth left-hand technique is *vibrato*.

HAMMER-ONS AND PULL-OFFS

HAMMER-ONS

Generally, a hammer-on is an ascending slur—where the pitch is raised. It is produced by playing one note, and while holding that note, sounding a second note by striking the fretboard with a finger of the left-hand. Stay close to the fret and use the tip of your finger. You will notice that in some cases, as in Exercises 44B (page 39) and 47 (page 41), we hammer-on to lower strings to make descending slurs. This is accomplished by tapping the lower string firmly with the left-hand finger.

Hammer-ons with open strings

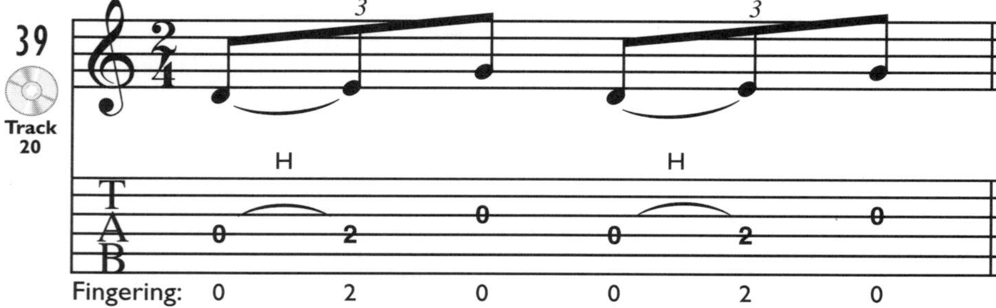

H = Hammer-on

Hammer-ons in a higher position on the neck

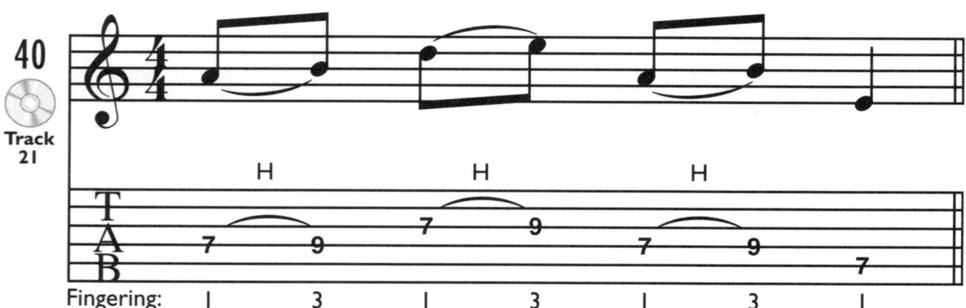

PULL-OFFS

A pull-off is a slur where the pitch is lowered. It is produced by playing a fretted note and then pulling the left-hand finger off the note to sound a lower note. If you are pulling-off from one fingered note to another fingered note, both fingers must be placed simultaneously. Often the 1st finger must *damp* or block an adjacent string to keep it from sounding when a note is pulled-off.

Pull-offs using open strings

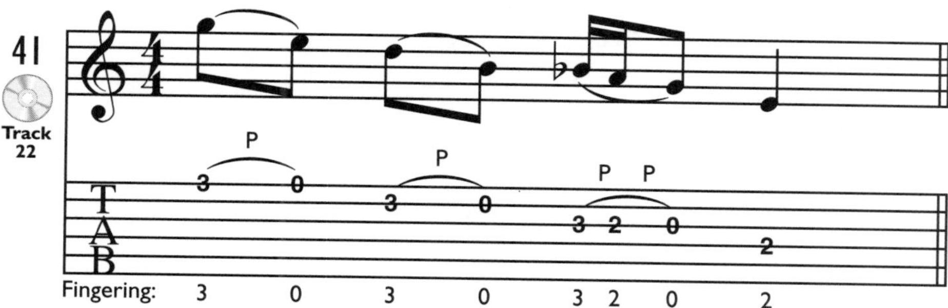

P = Pull-off

Pull-offs in a higher position on the neck

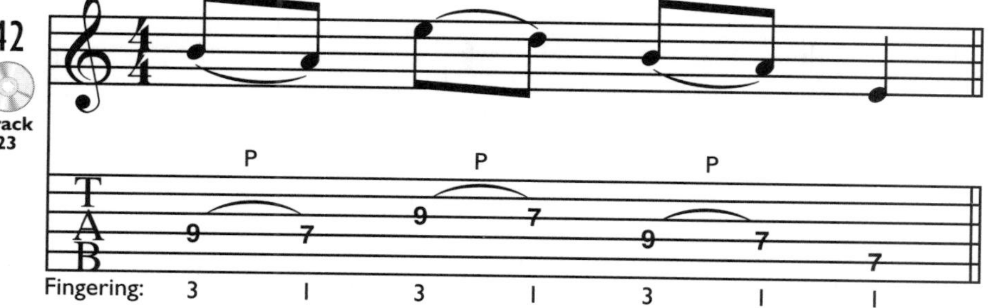

PHOTO • ROBERT KNIGHT

Eddie Van Halen

HAMMER-ON AND PULL-OFF EXERCISES

All the licks in Examples 43 and 44 use the A Minor Pentatonic scale starting on V. Notice the *grace note* in the second measure of Example 43A. A grace note is a very short note that precedes a main note. It is generally struck right on the beat.

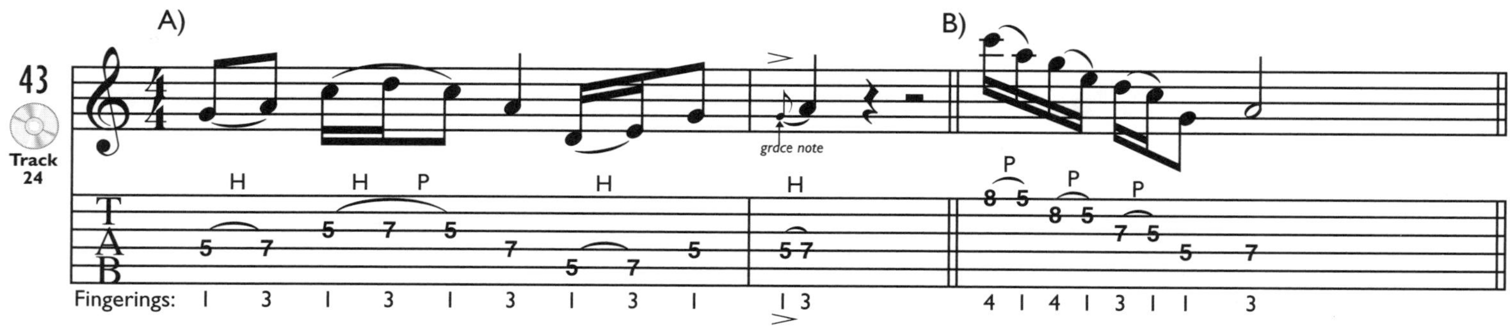

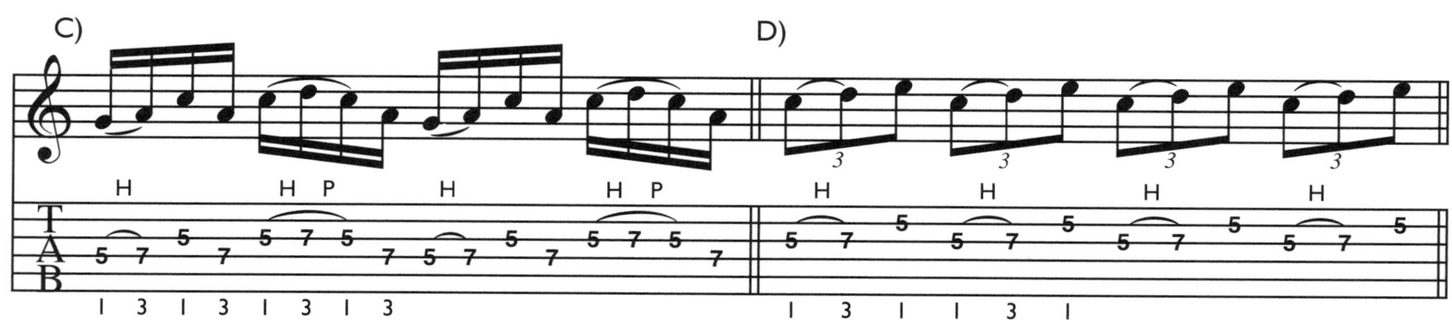

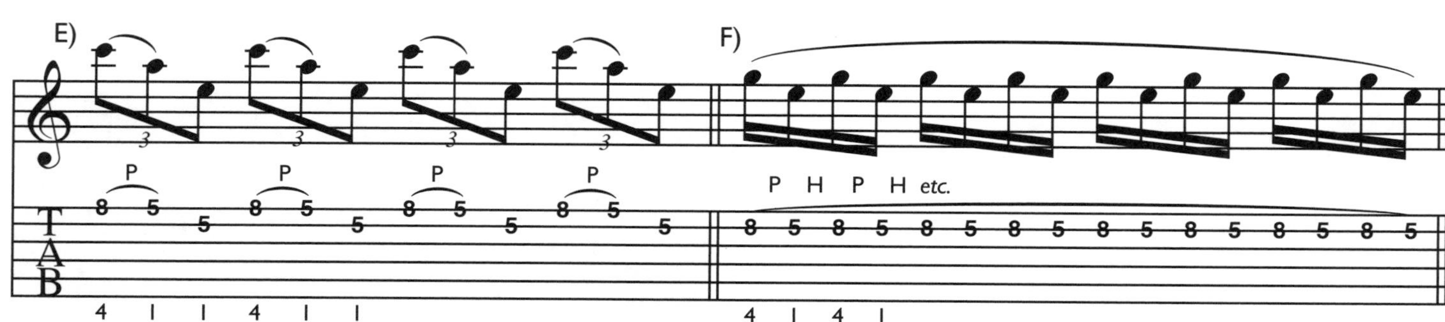

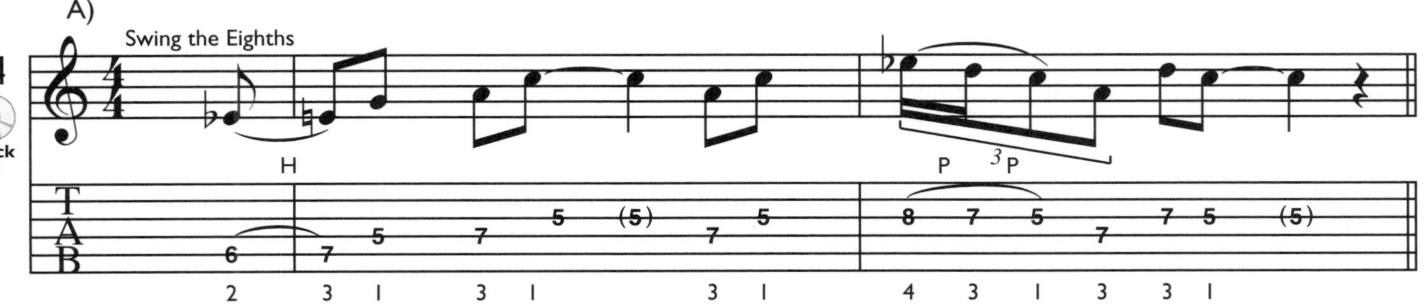

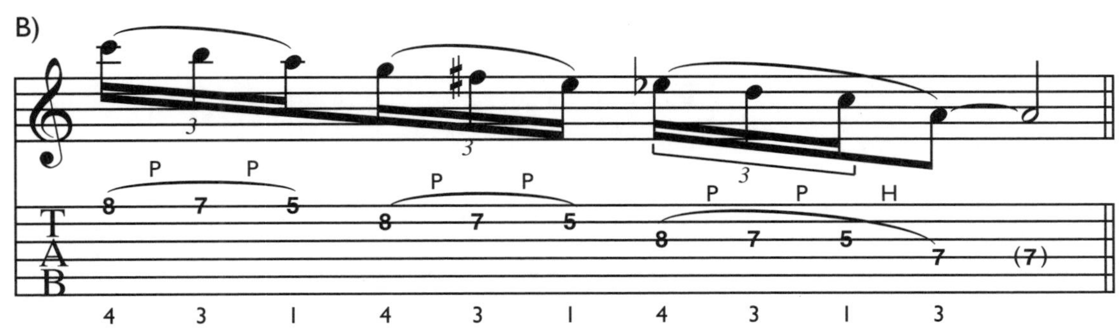

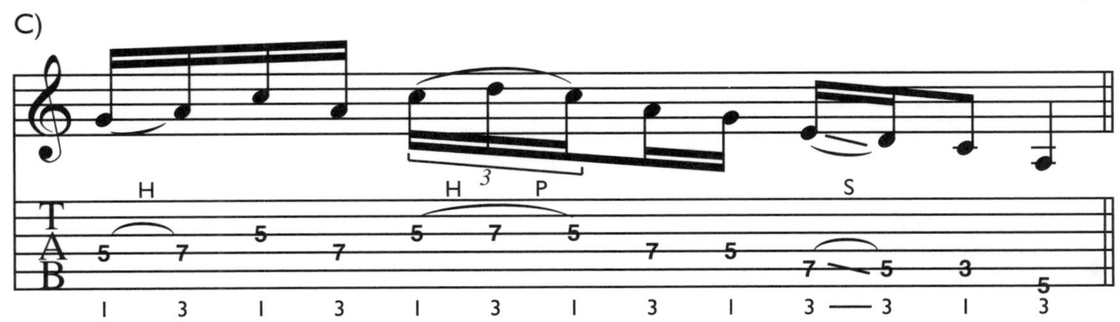

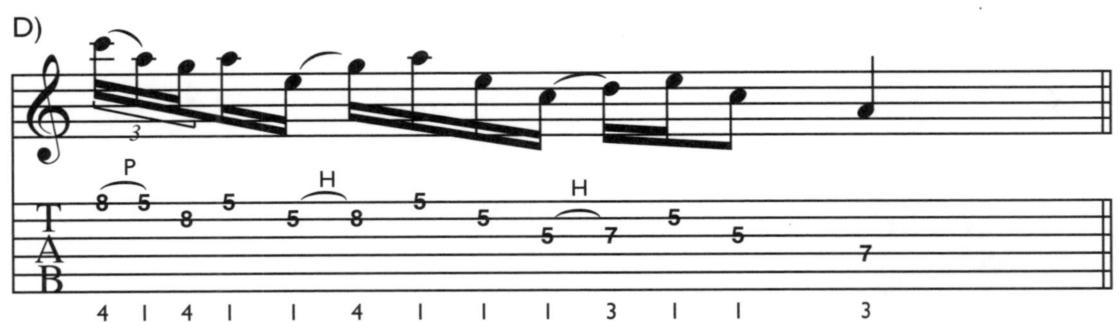

Now go back to page 35 and try Examples 37 and 38 using hammer-ons and pull-offs for a smoother and faster effect.

SLIDES

A slide is produced by playing a fretted note and sliding your finger up or down to the next note. If there is a slur sign, do not pick the second note in the slide. If the slide is to the first note of a lick, begin on a note one whole step (two frets) below the first note, and then slide up to it. For instance, if the note is an A on the 7th fret of the 4th string, begin the slide on the G on the 5th fret.

s = slide
/ = slide up
\ = slide down

PHOTO • PHOTOS BY FRED

Billy Gibbons of ZZ Top

VIBRATO

Vibrato is produced by playing a fretted note and causing it to waver in pitch by rapidly pushing the string back and forth or up and down. This sustains the note and imitates the sound of the human voice.

There are two vibrato techniques. In one, we place the finger firmly on the string and rock the wrist from left to right. In the other, we keep the hand still and move the finger to pull the string up and down. Try both of these techniques in the examples below.

∿∿∿ = vibrato

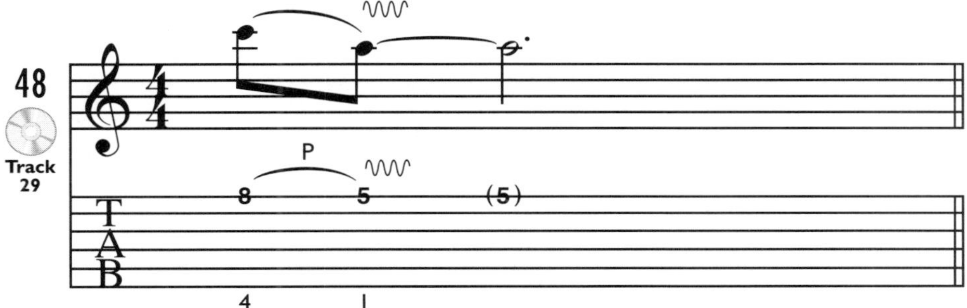

Randy Rhoades

BENDING

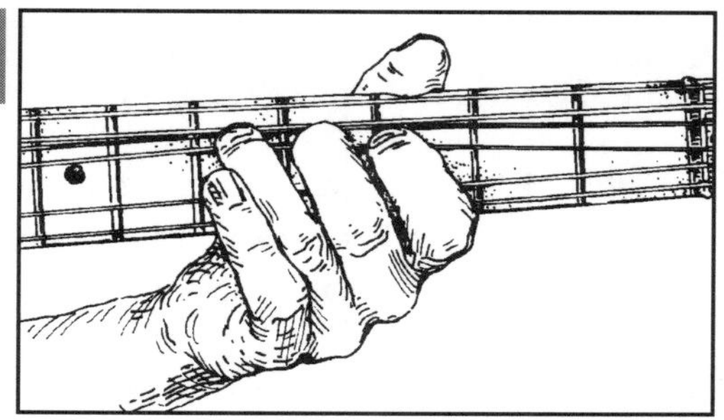

Bending is done by pushing the string up (towards the ceiling) or pulling it down (towards the floor) to create an effect of gliding up or down to the next note. Born in the blues, the bend is one of the most expressive rock techniques.

Generally, we bend notes up either a half step or a whole step, although wider bends are possible. Sometimes we bend a note and then release it back down to the original pitch. This is a called a *reverse bend*. Another important type of bend is the *prebend*. In a prebend, we bend the note up before plucking, pluck and then release.

Example 43A shows a half-step bend. 49B shows a whole-step bend. 49C shows a whole-step reverse bend.

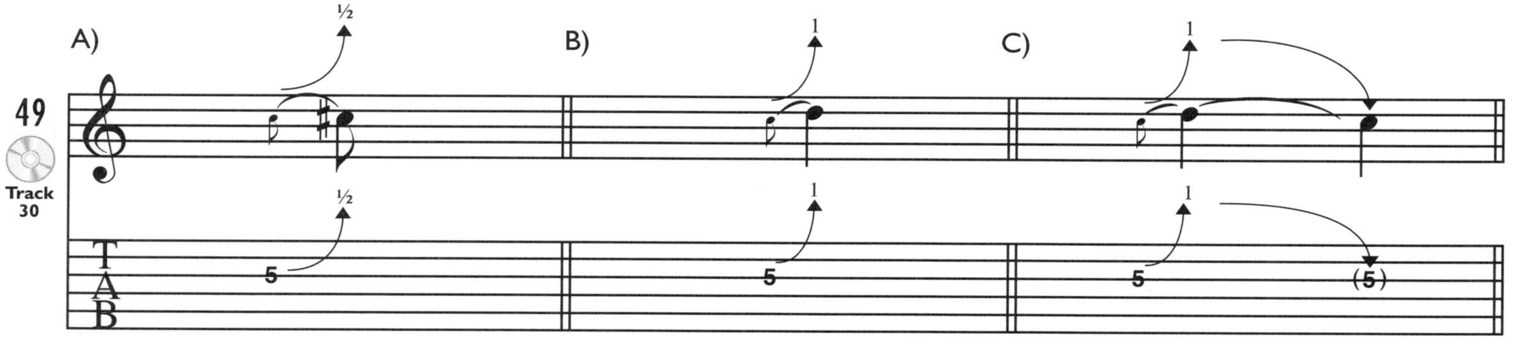

Example 50 shows a whole-step prebend.

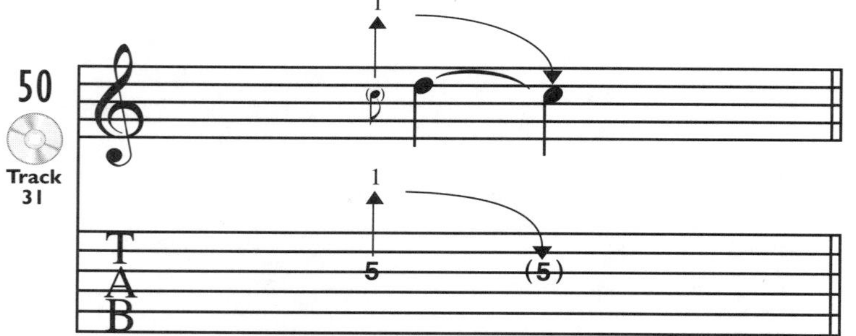

HALF-STEP BENDS
The ♭3 is sometimes bent a whole step.

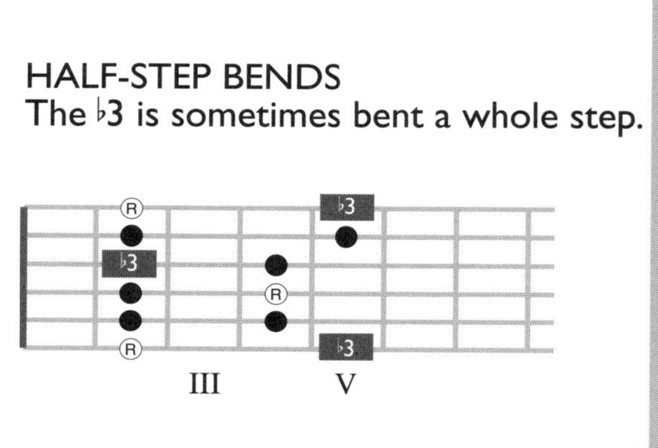

The diagrams on the right show the primary bending notes in the minor pentatonic scale. The 4 can be bent to sound as the 5 or ♭5, the ♭7 can be bent to sound as the root (I) and the ♭3 bent to sound as the ♮3. Practice bending in tune by first playing the pitch you are bending to normally. Then bend and match the pitch. Try adding vibrato. When bending with the 3rd finger, place the 1st and 2nd fingers on the string for support as in the drawing at the top of this page. When bending with the 4th finger, support with 2nd and 3rd fingers.

WHOLE-STEP BENDS
These are sometimes bent ½ step.

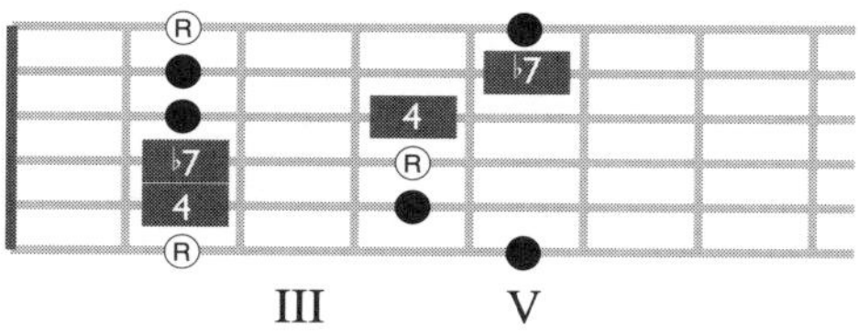

BENDING LICKS

Notice that all the bent notes in these examples are labeled (♭3, 4, ♭7) to help you learn how bending can be applied in the minor pentatonic scale.

Swing the eighths throughout.

UNISON BENDING

Unison bending is another common bending technique. It is done by bending a note on one string to match the pitch of a note sounding simultaneously on an adjacent string. This is usually done on the 1st and 2nd strings or 2nd and 3rd strings. For instance, while holding the A on the 5th fret of the 1st string, bend the G on the 8th fret of the 2nd string up one whole step to match the A.

Try playing the pentatonic scale on one string while bending the notes of the adjacent strings. Notice the difference in the two shapes due to the different intervals between the strings.

Bend the 2nd string to sound the same pitch as the 1st string. Use the 4th finger with the help of the 2nd and 3rd for added strength in the bends. Hold the 1st finger steady on its note.

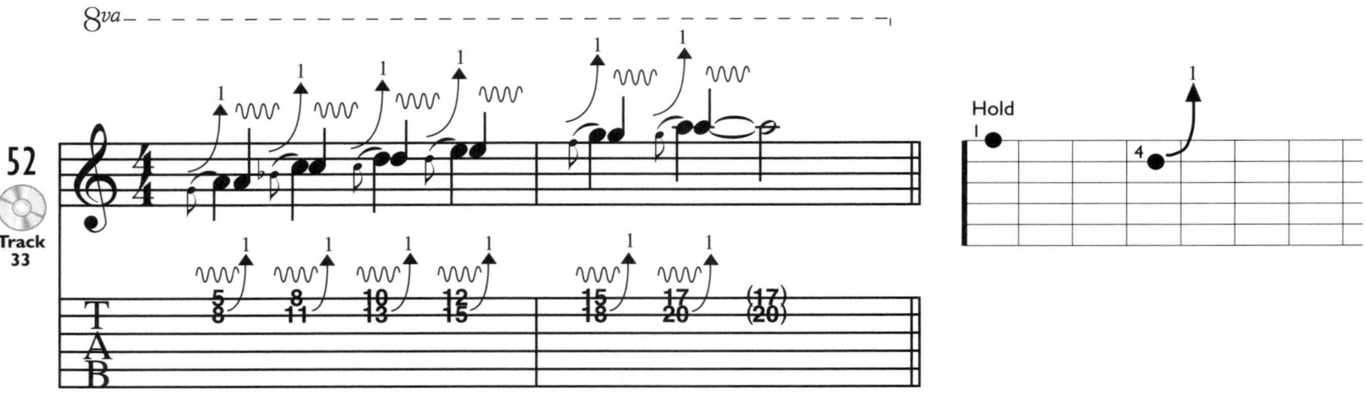

Bend the 3rd string to sound the same pitch as the 2nd string. Use the 3rd finger with the help of the 2nd. Notice that the shape of Example 53 on the fingerboard is different than the one in Example 52. That is because of the tuning of the guitar: the interval between the 2nd and 1st string is a 4th. Between the 3rd and 2nd string, the interval is only a 3rd.

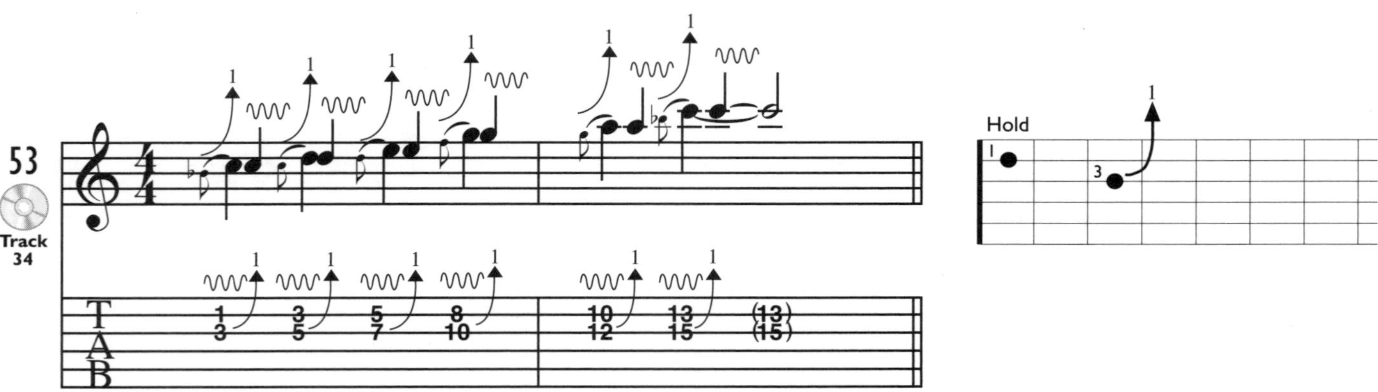

CHAPTER 6

Chords and Rhythm Guitar

TRIADS

A *chord* is a combination of three or more notes. Most chords are constructed by stacking notes that are an *interval of a 3rd* apart. For example, C to E is a 3rd (C_1 - D_2 - E_3), and E to G is a 3rd (E_1 - F_2 - G_3), so C - E - G is a three-note chord. We call these basic three-note chords *triads*. The most common types of triads are *major*, *minor* and *diminished* triads.

A major triad is built with 1 - 3 - 5 of a major scale. A minor triad is 1 - ♭3 - 5. A diminished triad is 1 - ♭3 - ♭5.

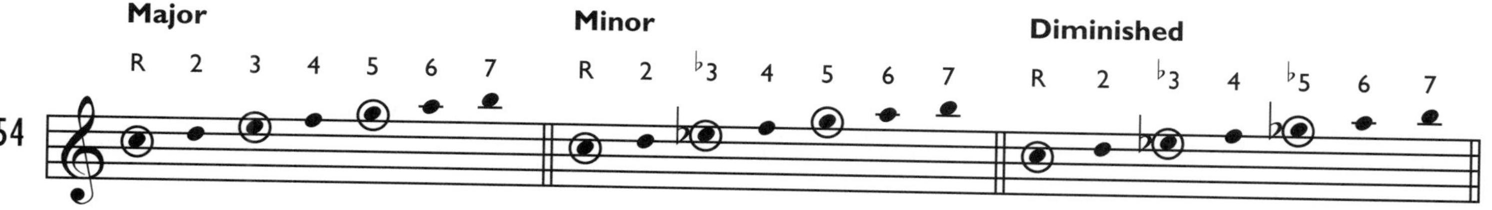

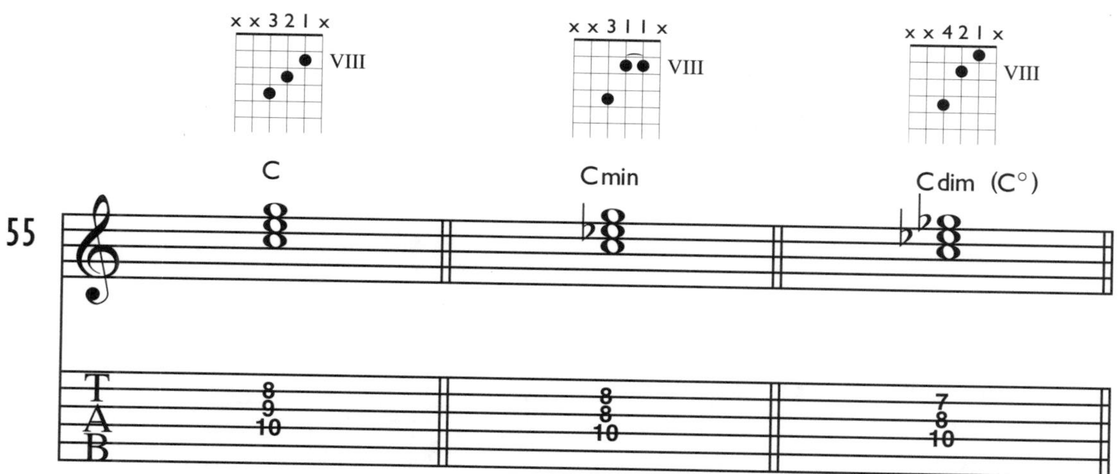

Chords can be played in many different *inversions* or *voicings*. In an inversion, the notes of the chord are rearranged so that a note other than the root is on the bottom (in the *bass*). Voicing refers to how the notes in the chord are distributed above the bass note. For instance, sometimes notes are *doubled*. That is to say, they appear twice or even three times in the chord voicing. Both inversions and voicings account for the various ways to play any particular chord, as you will see in the chord diagrams on pages 48 and 49.

BASIC DIATONIC HARMONY

Chords in songs are usually constructed from the scale on which the song is based (from a particular key). When we talk about these chords, we use a Roman numeral to identify the scale degree on which the chord is built. Major chords are indicated by upper case and minor chords by lower case numerals. A diminished chord is indicated by a "°" and lowercase Roman numerals.

Here is what happens when we build a triad on every note of the C Major scale.

56
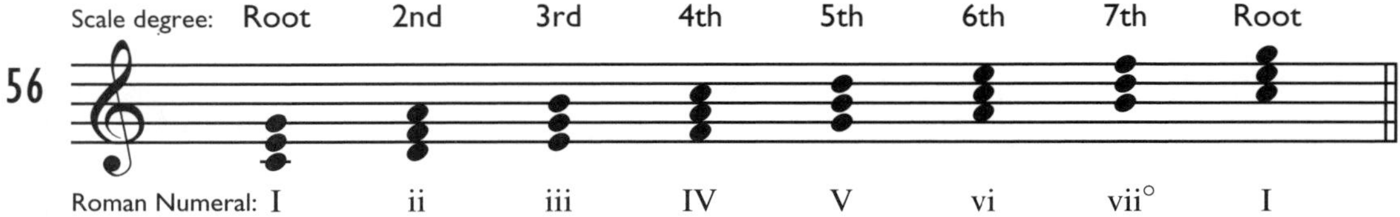

Notice the Roman numerals. They indicate that I, IV and V are major triads, ii, iii and vi are minor, and vii° is diminished. We call these the *diatonic chords*. This is true in every major key!

THE THREE PRINCIPLE CHORDS

The three most important chords in music are the major chords on I, IV and V. We call these *principle chords*. Here are the notes of the E Major scale, including Roman numerals showing the triad types built on them, and the three principle chords for the key of E.

I	ii	iii	IV	V	vi	vii°
E	**F♯**	**G♯**	**A**	**B**	**C♯**	**D♯**

The Three Principle Chords in E Major:

I	IV	V
E Major	**A Major**	**B Major**

THE DOMINANT 7TH CHORD

Frequently, the V chord has another tone added a 3rd above the 5th, which is a ♭7 above the root (1 - 3 - 5 - ♭7). This is a called a *dominant 7th* chord (V7). The example on the right shows the V7 chord in the key of E, which is B7.

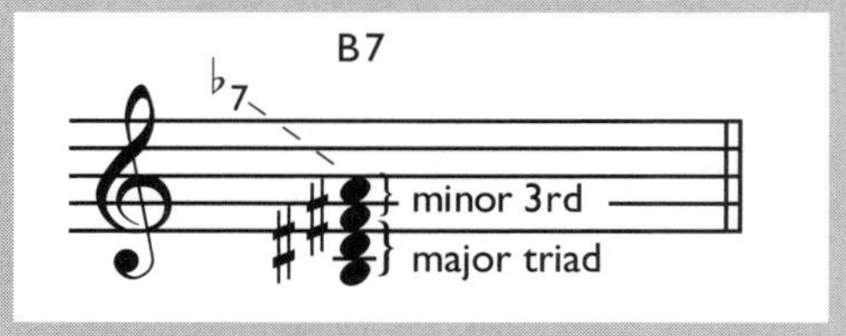

OTHER COMMONLY USED CHORDS

DIATONIC

The minor chord built on vi is used frequently. In the key of E, vi is a C♯ Minor triad.

NON-DIATONIC

Very often, chords are used from outside of the scale. These are *non-diatonic* chords. The most common of these are major chords built on the ♭3, ♭6 and ♭7 of the scale. In the key of E these chords are as follows:

♭III	♭VI	♭VII
G Major	**C Major**	**D Major**

SUMMARY OF THE BASIC CHORD GROUP

Thousands of songs have been written by manipulating this basic chord group. Here is a quick summary:

The Principle Chords: I IV V (or V7)

Other Common Chords: vi ♭III ♭VI ♭VII

Sometimes chords built on the other major scale degrees are used: ii, iii and vii°. The diminished chord built on the 7th degree (vii°) is rarely used in rock music because the sound is so close to that of the V7, which is far more common.

You should learn to name all of these chords in any key. Here they are in the keys of A Major and G Major.

In the Key of A

I	ii	iii	IV	V	vi	vii°
A	**Bmin**	**C♯min**	**D**	**E**	**F♯min**	**G♯dim**

♭III	♭VI	♭VII
C Major	**F Major**	**G Major**

In the Key of G

I	ii	iii	IV	V	vi	vii°
G	**Amin**	**Bmin**	**C**	**D**	**Emin**	**F♯dim**

♭III	♭VI	♭VII
B♭ Major	**E♭ Major**	**F Major**

BASIC CHORD FORMS

This page and page 49 show diagrams for what we call the *basic chords* on the guitar. They are listed by key, with the simpler keys first. The I, IV, V7 and vi are shown for each of these keys. Some of these chords are *open chords* (they include open strings) and some of them are best played as *barre chords* and may be a little more difficult at first. Barre chords are played by laying the 1st finger flat across the strings while the other fingers play a shape above it (see page 54, the section on "Movable Chords").

Numbers above the diagrams are fingerings. An "x" means not to strike, or to mute, that string. "0" means the string is played open. The numbers and letters below the diagrams are chord degrees that can be used as *bass* notes. A bass note is the lowest note you play in a chord. An "R" stands for a root bass note, "5" and "3" are often alternate bass notes. A note in parentheses (●) means a left hand finger must move to play an alternate bass note. Ordinarily the root is in the bass. Some forms can be inversions, and have alternate chord tones other than the root in the bass. Notice that sometimes there are alternative fingerings for the same chord. The best option is based on the context. A Roman numeral next to a chord diagram indicates a fret number.

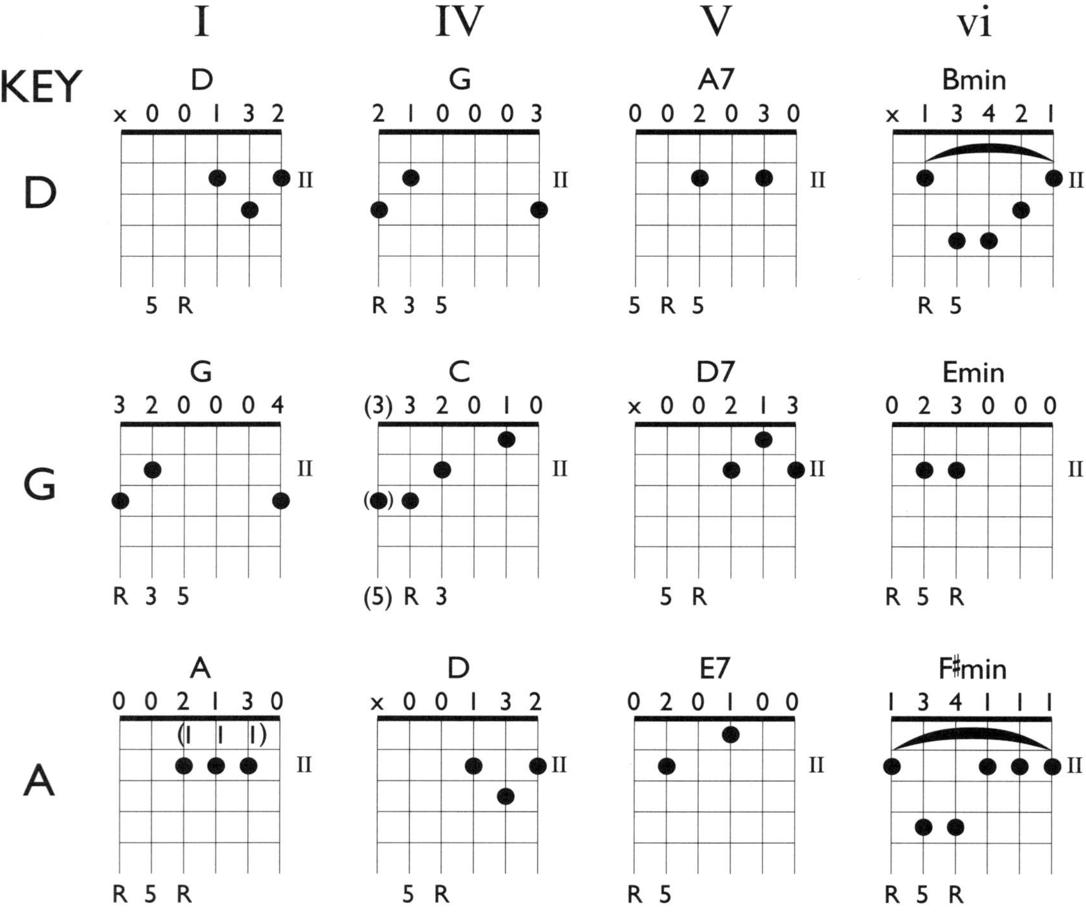

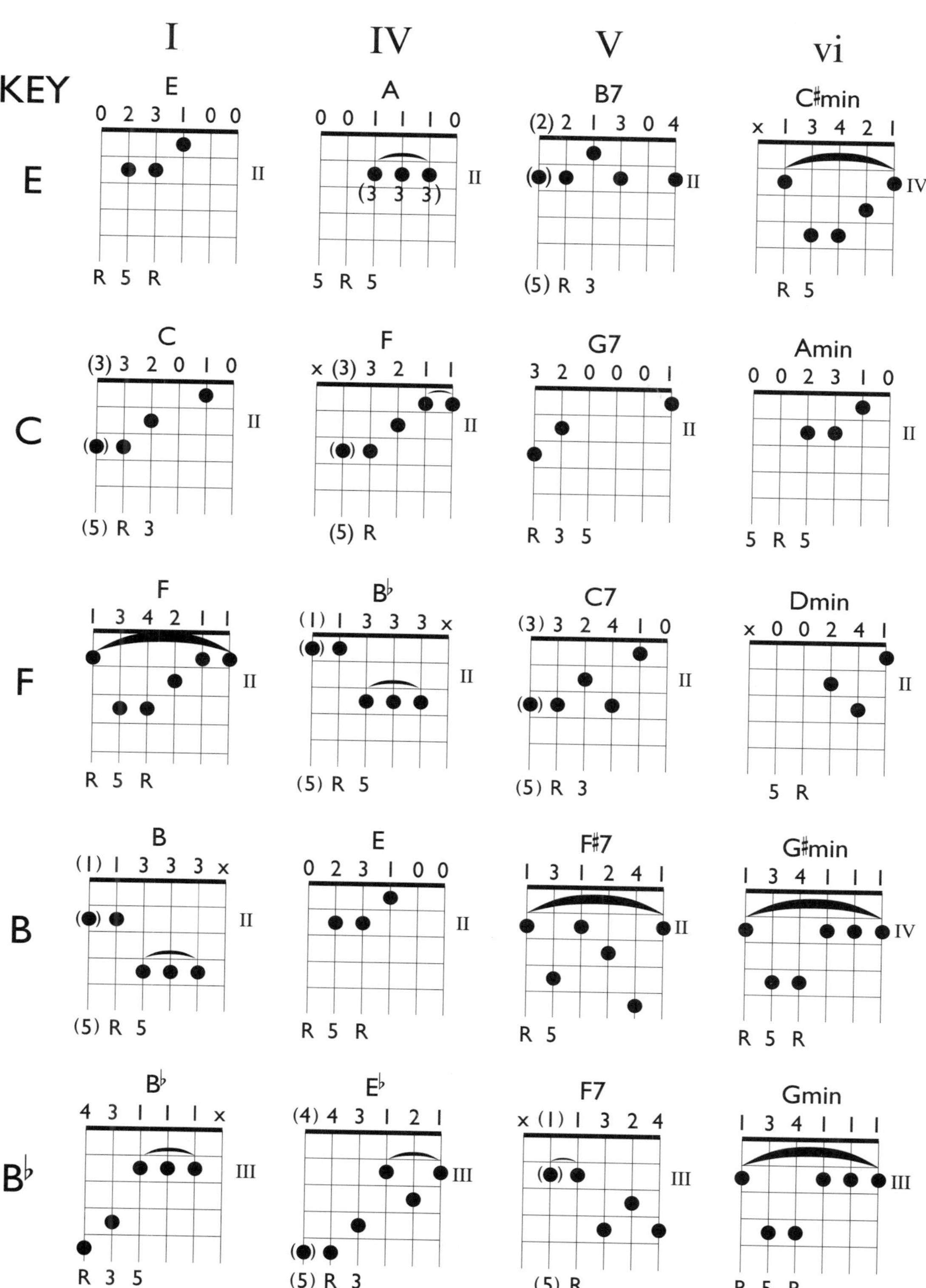

I
IV
V
vi
KEY
E
E
0 2 3 1 0 0
R 5 R
A
0 0 1 1 1 0
(3 3 3)
5 R 5
B7
(2) 2 1 3 0 4
(5) R 3
C♯min
x 1 3 4 2 1
R 5
C
C
(3) 3 2 0 1 0
(5) R 3
F
x (3) 3 2 1 1
(5) R
G7
3 2 0 0 0 1
R 3 5
Amin
0 0 2 3 1 0
5 R 5
F
F
1 3 4 2 1 1
R 5 R
B♭
(1) 1 3 3 3 x
(5) R 5
C7
(3) 3 2 4 1 0
(5) R 3
Dmin
x 0 0 2 4 1
5 R
B
B
(1) 1 3 3 3 x
(5) R 5
E
0 2 3 1 0 0
R 5 R
F♯7
1 3 1 2 4 1
R 5
G♯min
1 3 4 1 1 1
R 5 R
B♭
B♭
4 3 1 1 1 x
R 3 5
E♭
(4) 4 3 1 2 1
(5) R 3
F7
x (1) 1 3 2 4
(5) R
Gmin
1 3 4 1 1 1
R 5 R
II
III
IV

RHYTHM GUITAR

Rhythm guitar playing is truly an art. It is an essential part of a complete guitarist's vocabulary. Rhythm playing is usually accomplished using chords or combinations of chords, double stops (two notes at a time) and single note lines. The rhythm guitar supports and accompanies the vocal part or other lead parts. It must be solid, in time and help move the song forward. The key word is *rhythm*. One must learn to work with the drummer, bass player and often the keyboard player to provide a band with a solid *rhythm section*. Every lead player is sometimes part of the rhythm section!

Besides learning chords, the guitarist must learn many left- and right-hand techniques that add interest and intensity to a rhythm guitar part. Let's talk about the right hand.

In general, when learning to play rhythm patterns, use down strokes with the pick for the first part of the beat and up strokes for the second. Later this can be varied for the purposes of shifting *accents* (emphasis).

Remember, another useful right-hand technique is to damp the strings near the bridge with the side of the right hand palm to mute or muffle the sound. You must touch the strings very close to the bridge or you will loose the sound completely. This is called palm muting (PM) (see page 27).

Practice the rhythm patterns in Examples 57 through 61 using open chords, following the picking indications. Notice that the Roman numeral designation for each chord is given. Try to be aware of them as you play. It is important to learn the sound of each of these common chord progressions.

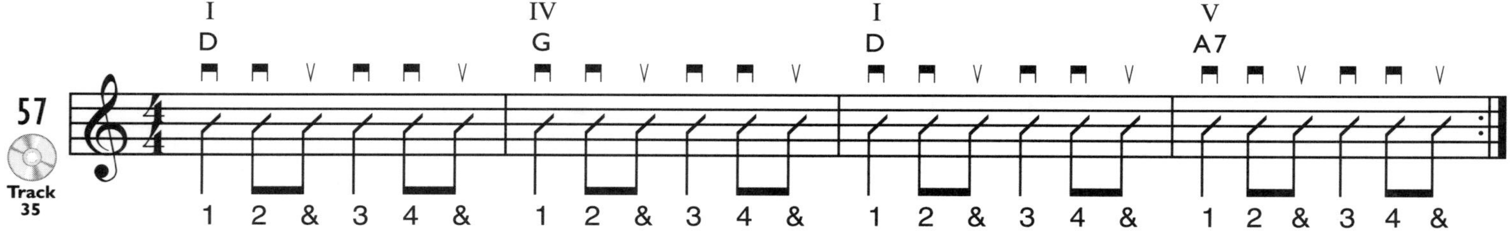

Swing the eighths in Example 58.

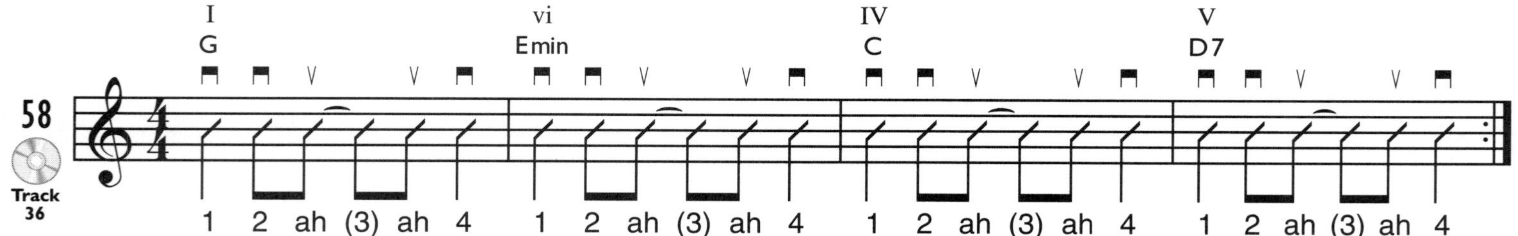

Swing the eighths in Example 59.

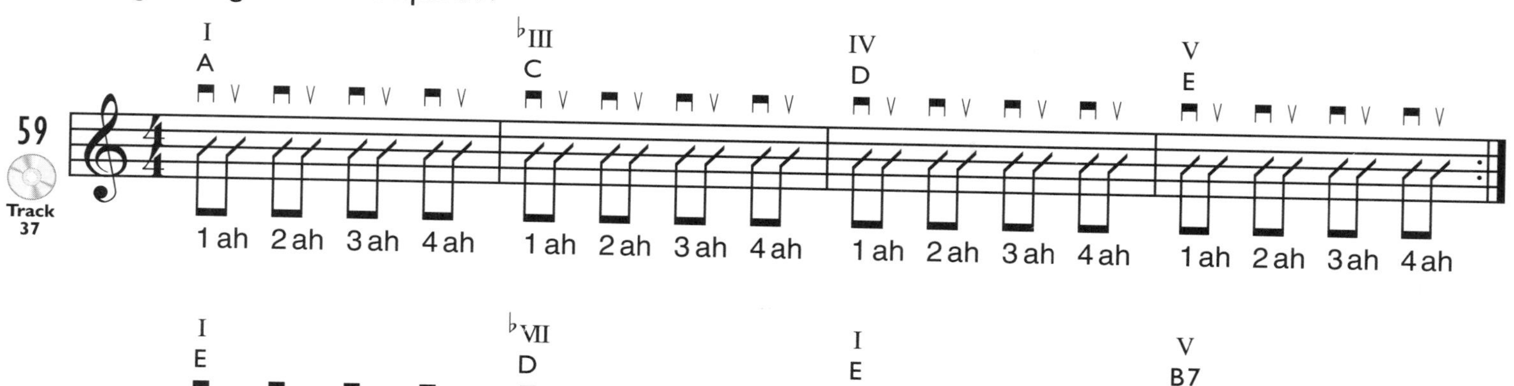

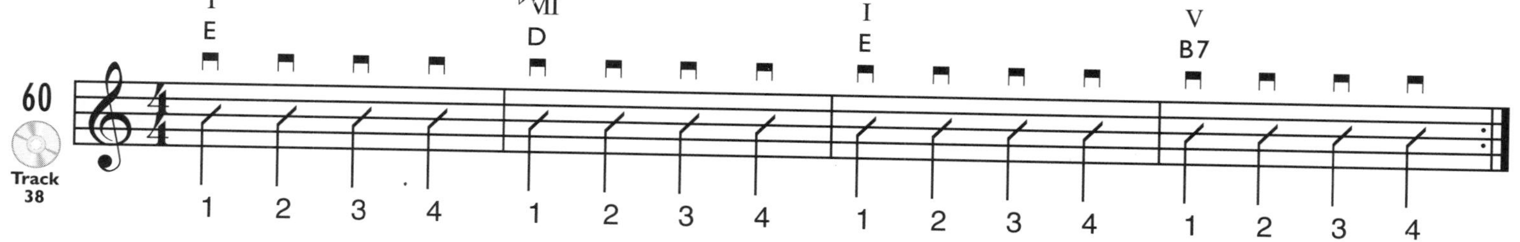

Straight eighths

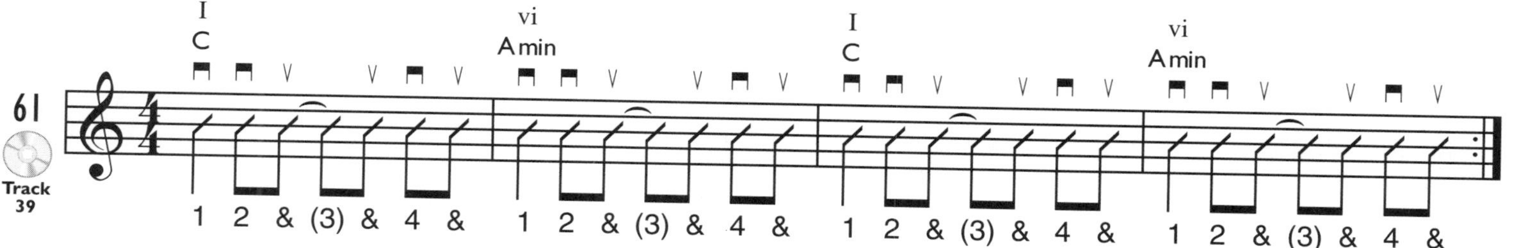

Keith Richards

LEFT-HAND DAMPING

You may have noticed that the sound of a chord will continue as long as you maintain constant pressure with your left hand. This is not always a desirable effect, especially on the electric guitar. Occasional silences and spaces add more interest to the rhythmic pulse.

This brings us to *left-hand damping*. By choosing *specific moments* to apply pressure or to release pressure with the left hand, even simple rhythms can have much more punch and rhythmic drive. We can immediately release left-hand pressure on the fretted notes of a chord to stop the sound completely. Make sure your hand remains in contact with the strings or the sound of the open strings will ring out. These *staccato* (shortened) chords look like this and are used in Example 64.

Releasing left-hand pressure when you strike the strings results in a rhythmic *chuck*. The chuck is indicated and is sometimes called a *cut*.

How you use your left hand can determine whether you strike a chord and let it ring, strike a chord and stop the sound quickly (staccato) or strike the muted strings with the right hand (chuck or cut).

Try some of the patterns that follow to practice left-hand damping. Sometimes the right hand can help out with damping the open strings in open chords. Try using different combinations and sequences of the basic chord group as you practice rhythm playing in different keys. Try soloing over these progressions, too. Have fun!

RHYTHM GUITAR EXAMPLES WITH LEFT-HAND DAMPING

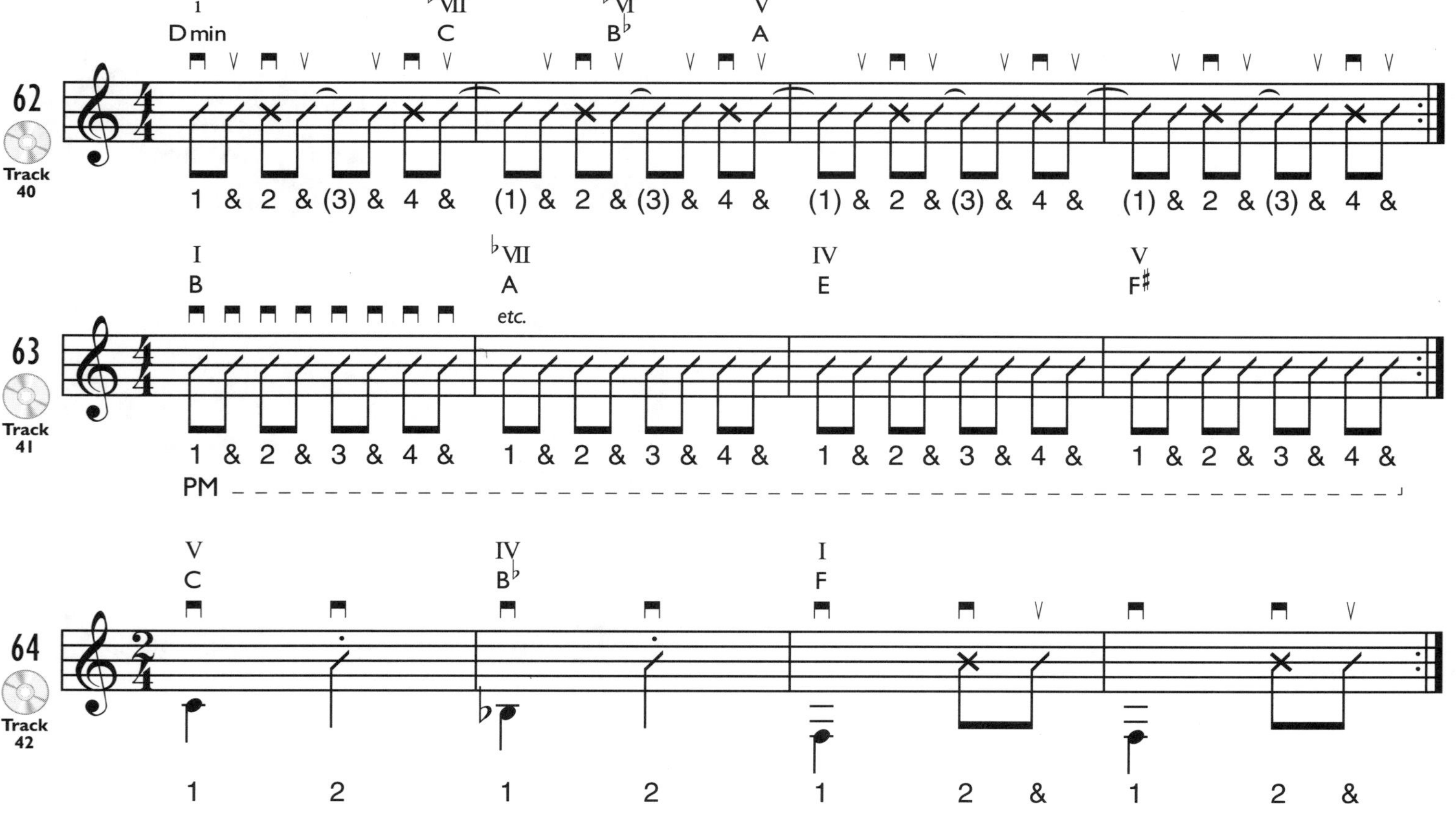

SLASH CHORDS

Whenever a chord symbol is written with a slash (/) a note other than the root is played in the bass. It may even be a note from outside the chord. For instance, C/B means to play a C chord with a B in the bass. This is called a *slash chord*. In other words, you are adding a bass note that is not normally used under the chord. This often happens in situations in which there is a descending bass line under a relatively static harmony.

Examples 65 and 66 also have some complex chords that are easy to play on the guitar because of the addition of certain open strings to our familiar voicings, such as the FMaj7 (1 - 3 - 5 - 7 = F - A - C - E) and FMaj7♭5 (1 - 3 - ♭5 - 7 = F - A - C♭ - E) in Example 65. The diagrams above the chord symbols will tell you the position and fingering of these chords.

RHYTHM GUITAR EXAMPLES WITH SLASH CHORDS

Notice that we use the left hand thumb, indicated "T," to finger some of the bass notes in Example 65. Remember to let your hand return to it's normal position afterwards.

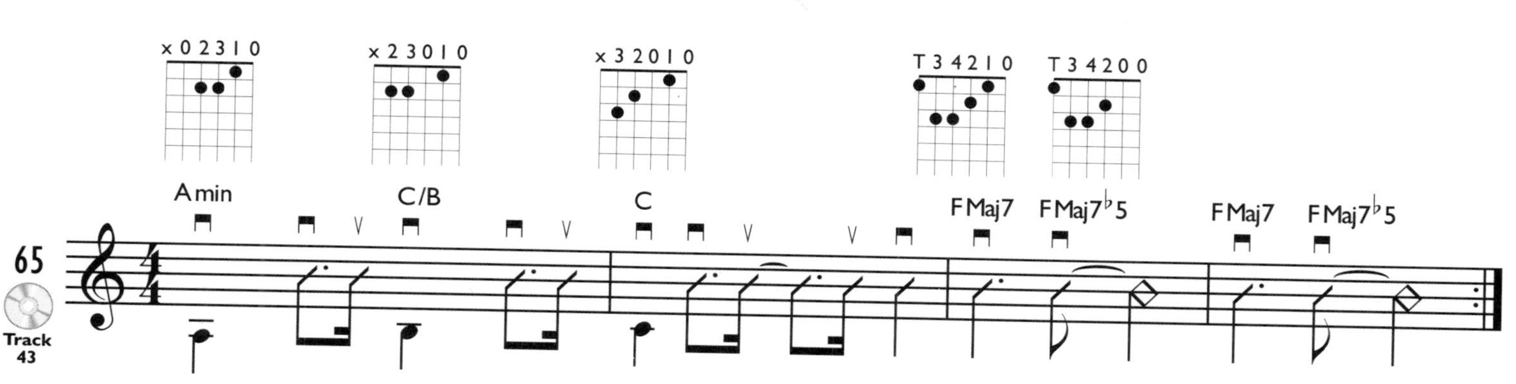

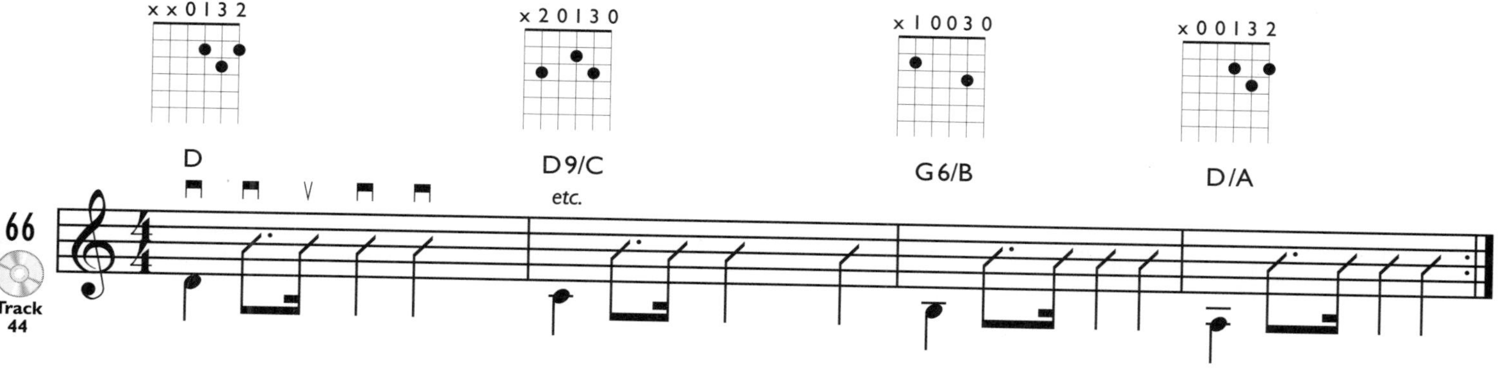

MOVABLE CHORDS

There are many chord forms which are *movable*. They are movable because all the notes are fingered (no open strings are involved) and therefore move as a unit up or down the fingerboard. Moving the form to a different fret gives the same type of chord with a different root. The power chords you learned in Chapter 3 and the barre chords you have learned in this chapter are movable chords.

The best way to learn these chords is in groups that have roots on either the 5th or 6th strings. The chords will be named by the fret on which the root falls. Chords with their root on the 6th string are called Root ⑥ chords and are based on "E" type chords. In other words, we create barre chords using E, E7, Emin and Emin7 chord shapes. Chords with their root on the 5th string are called Root ⑤ chords and are based on "A" type chords. In other words, we create barre chords using A, A7, Amin and Amin7 chord shapes. Always remember the order of the chromatic scale as you move the forms up and down the neck, just as you did with power chords.

Because these chords have no open strings, the left hand has complete control of damping or letting the notes ring. Also remember you don't need to always strike all the strings of the chord. You may want to strike only the lower notes, or only the higher notes. Variations of this type add a lot of interest to chord playing.

The following diagrams will help you locate roots for all the movable chords.

Root ⑥ names for E Forms

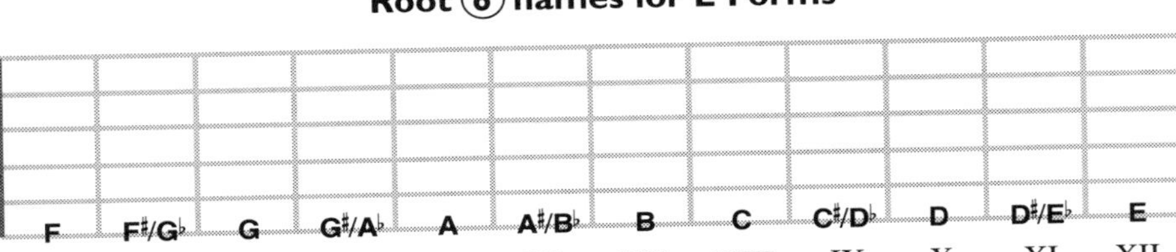

Root ⑤ names for A Forms

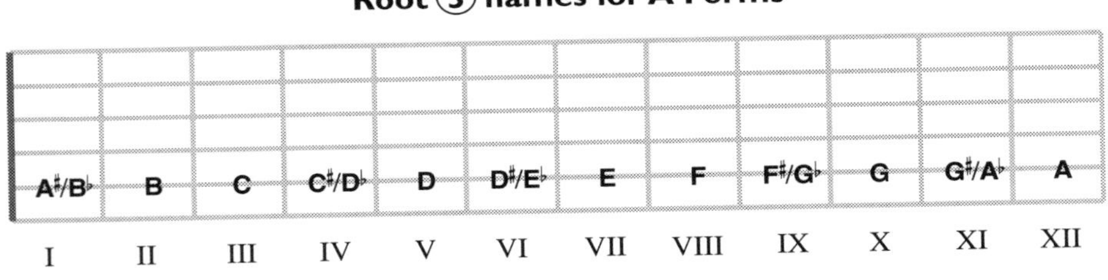

⑥ = A circled number represents a string

A good left-hand position is extremely important for making a good barre chord. Keep your thumb behind the neck and your wrist low. Keep your 1st finger straight so it frets each string properly. Be sure to keep the finger close to the fret and move your elbow in towards your side to use more of the left side of your finger and improve your leverage.

The diagrams that follow show Root ⑥ and Root ⑤ forms for four types of chords: major (1 - 3 - 5), minor (1 - ♭3 - 5), dominant 7th (1 - 3 - 5 - ♭7) and minor 7th (1 - ♭3 - 5 - ♭7).

(●) = Optional note

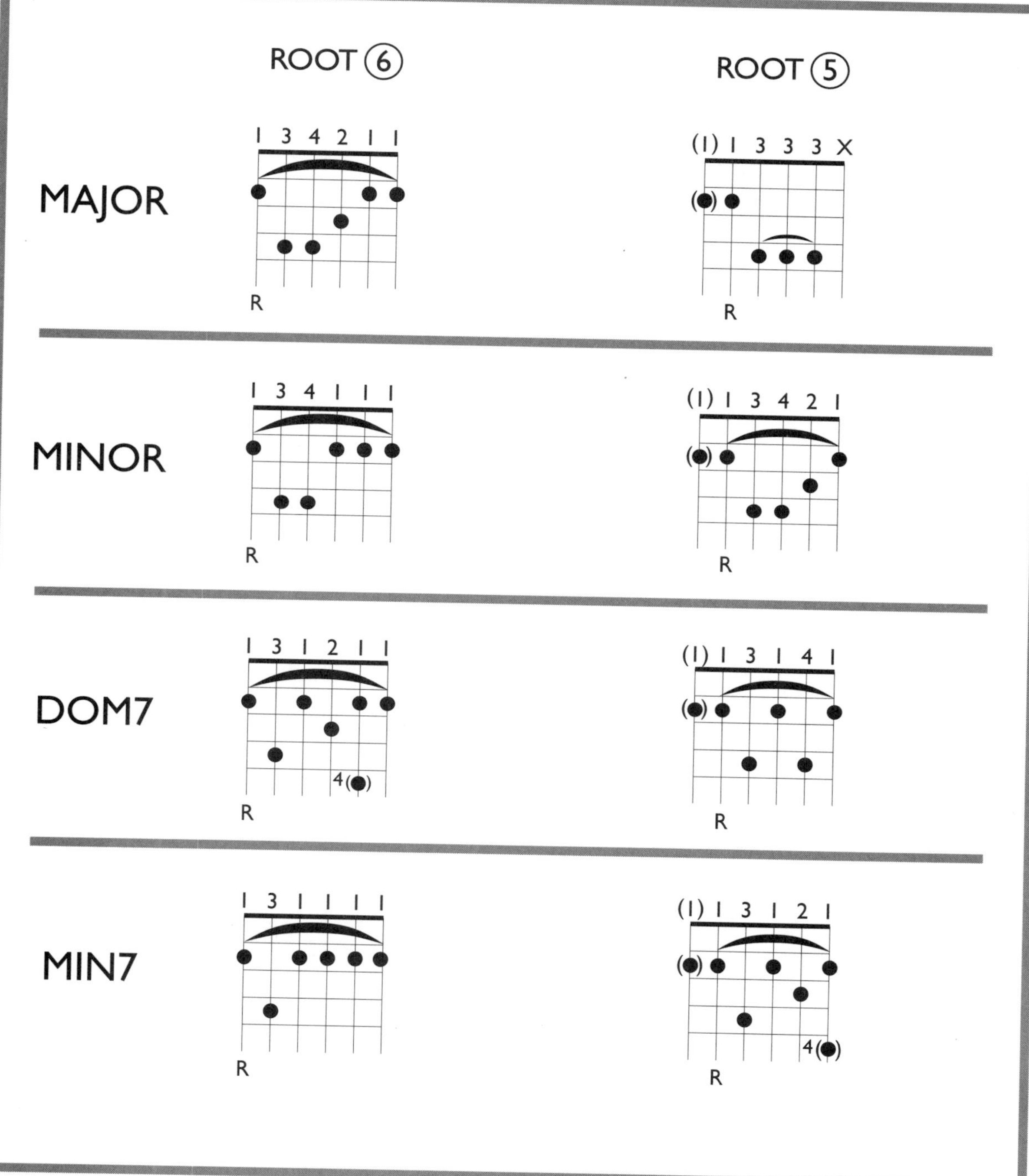

PRINCIPLE CHORDS (I, IV AND V) ON THE FINGERBOARD

When using a Root ⑥ chord to play the I chord of a key, the IV chord will be a Root ⑤ chord at the same fret, and the V chord will be a Root ⑤ chord two frets higher.

In the Key of A

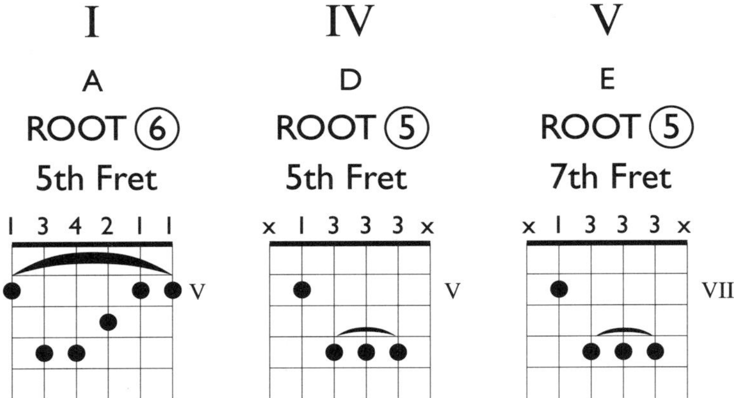

When using a Root ⑤ chord to play the I chord of a key, the IV chord will be a Root ⑥ chord two frets lower, and the V chord will be a Root ⑥ chord on the same fret as the I.

In the Key of E

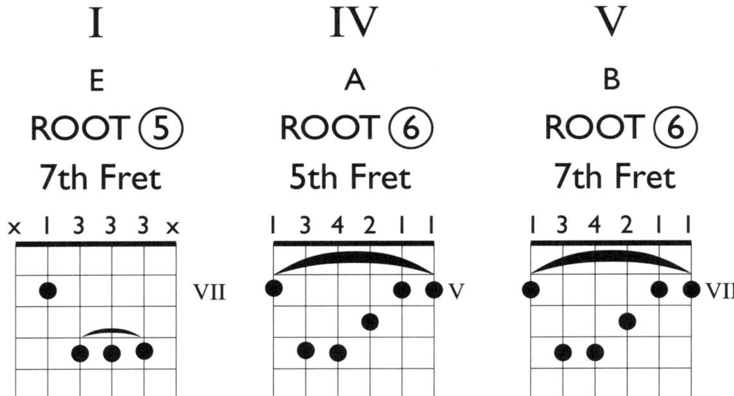

Use movable chords for the following examples. Find the proper form to use for each chord based on the fret indicated. Pay attention to the *tempo* (speed) or style suggested for each example. Try to *transpose* (change the key) by starting on different frets.

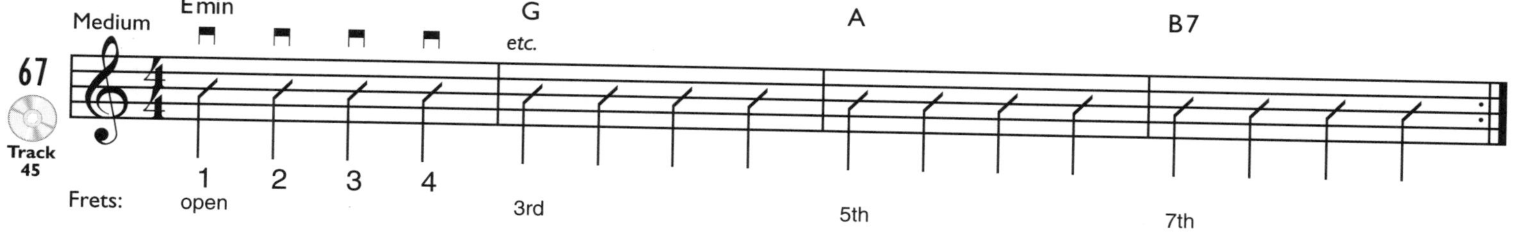

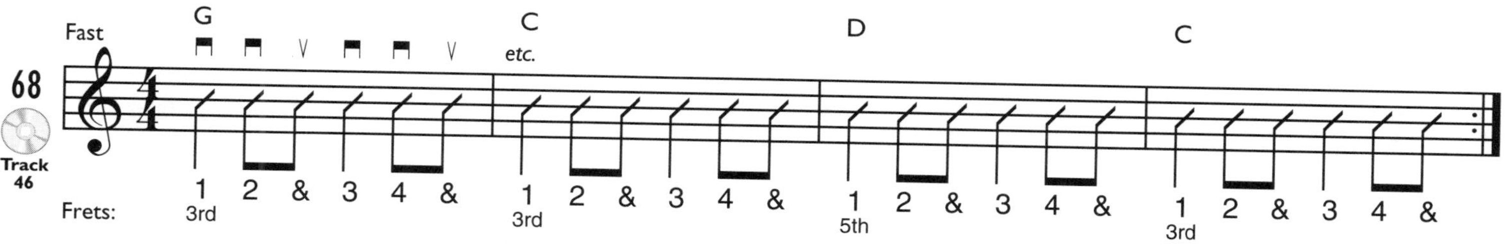

Swing the eighths in Example 69.

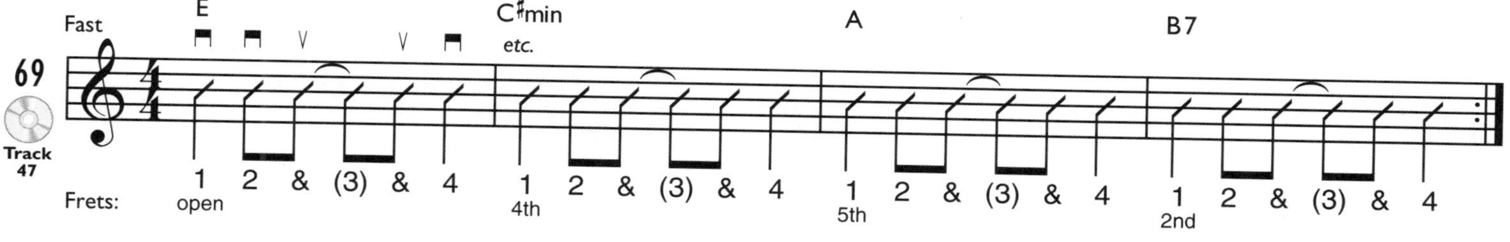

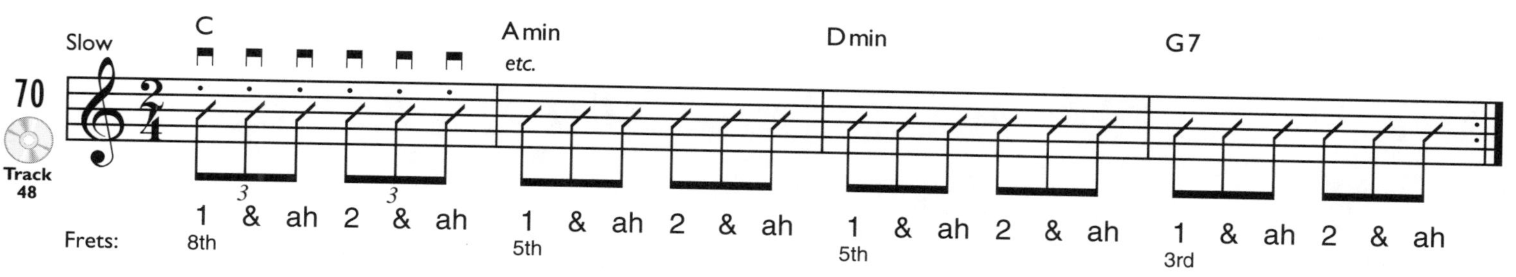

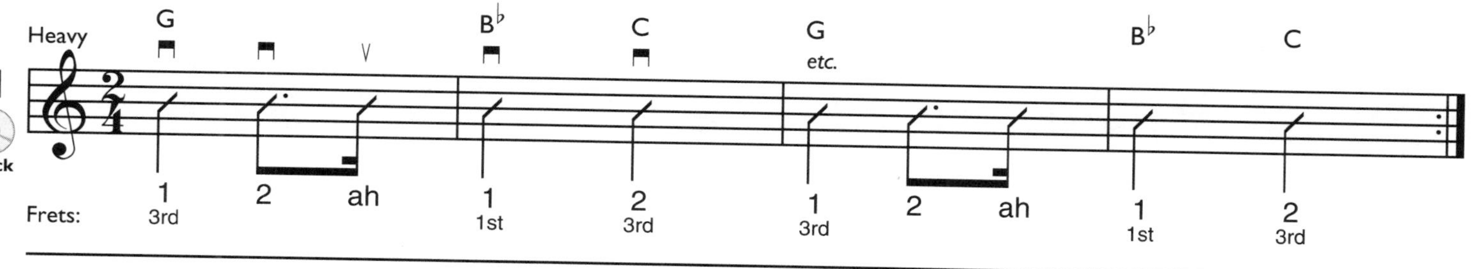

RHYTHM & BLUES PATTERNS

One of the most common sounds, especially in early rock, is the rhythm & blues (R&B) riff. We play double-stop 5ths on adjacent strings and move the pinky on and off the upper string to alternate between the 5th and 6th, and sometimes the ♭7, of the chord.

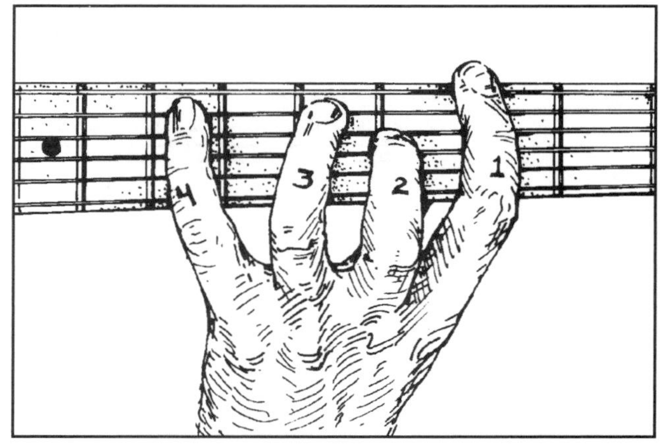

The diagrams below show the pattern with the root on the 6th string and the root on the 5th string.

ROOT ⑥

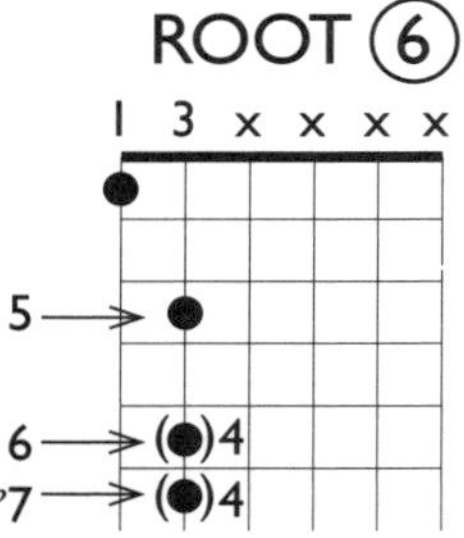

ROOT ⑤

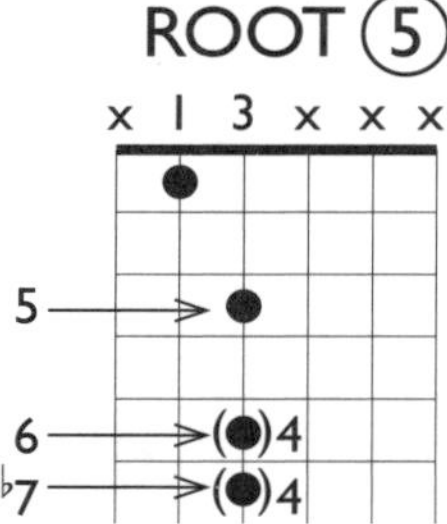

(●) = A note added on with the 4th finger

PHOTO • ROBERT KNIGHT

Stevie Ray Vaughn

In the style of Chuck Berry

Example 73 has a *shuffle* feel. That means there is a feeling of three pulses per beat. In this case, it is notated in triplets. It is also common to find songs with this feel written in straight eighths, as in Example 72. The indication "Shuffle," however, would be enough to tell us that we should swing the eighths and play them as notated below.

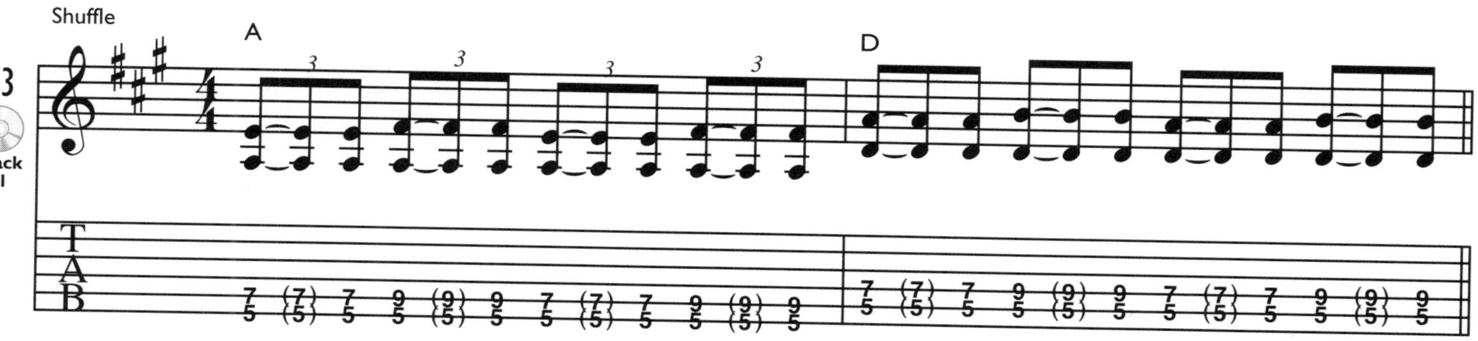

TRIADS

We know the term *triad* as a basic theoretical term referring to stacking three notes on top of each other in 3rds. In another context, *triad* refers to any three-note voicing—no matter what kind of chord it is. Great players such as Eddie Van Halen, Jimi Hendrix, Keith Richards and others have made extensive use of triads.

The triads being introduced here are major chords on the 4th, 3rd and 2nd strings, but two of them are in inversion. In other words, the lowest note is something other than the root. In 1st inversion, the 3rd (3) is the lowest note. In 2nd inversion, the 5th (5) is the lowest note.

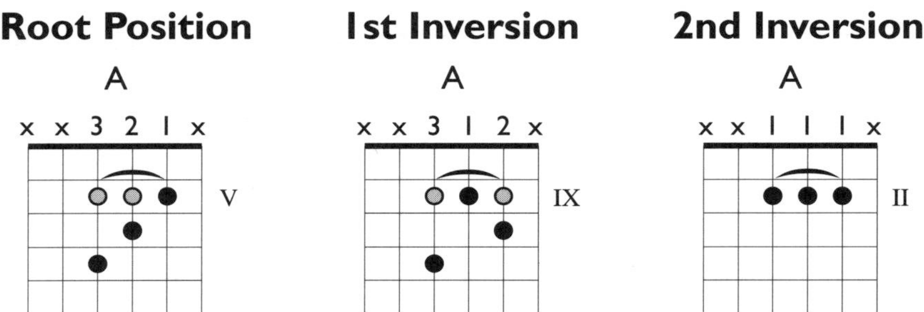

○ = A note being held in a barre, but not played.

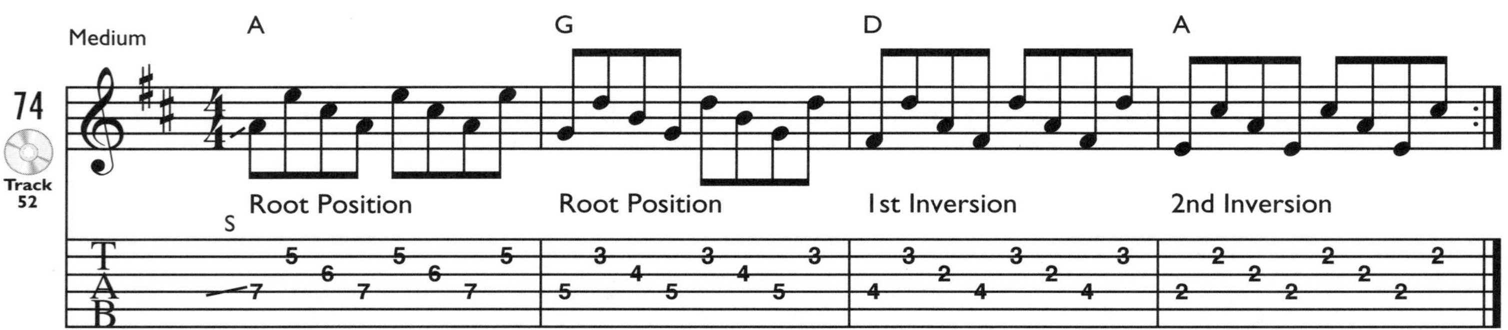

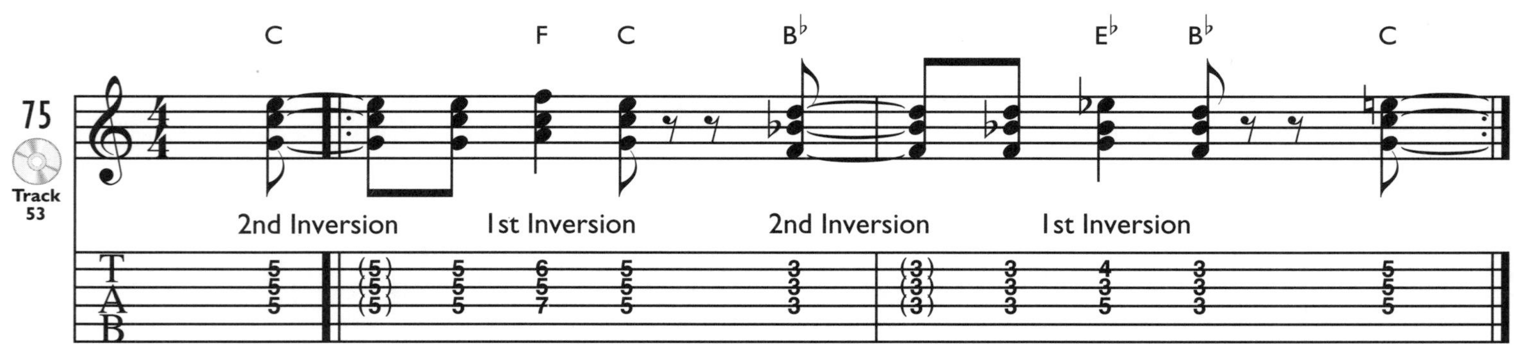

CHAPTER 7

More Minor Pentatonics

MINOR PENTATONIC SCALE FINGERING #2

As you know, the minor pentatonic scale is a five-note scale that contains the scale degrees: 1 - ♭3 - 4 - 5 - ♭7. Remember that "1" refers to any root note, and this scale can be played through all octaves and in all positions on the guitar.

We can play the same note in more than one place on the finger board. In other words, the same octave can be found in a different position on a different string. Scale fingerings or patterns help us to find the proper notes in all areas of the fingerboard. Try playing a pentatonic scale on one string and you will become more aware of the spacing of the notes in the scale and more used to playing up and down the neck of the guitar.

To move from Fingering #1 up the neck to Fingering #2, we move the 1st finger to the 4th string root note that was previously played by the 3rd finger. To move from Fingering #1 to Fingering #2 in the key of A, we move the 1st finger from the 4th string, 5th fret to the 4th string, 7th fret, where there is a root note.

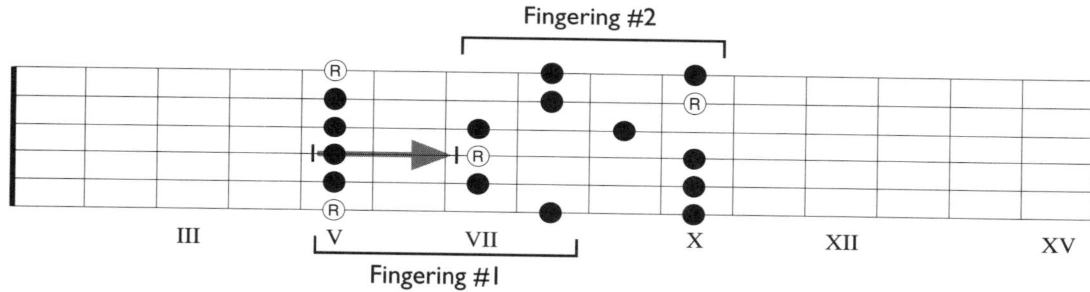

A MINOR PENTATONIC FINGERING #2

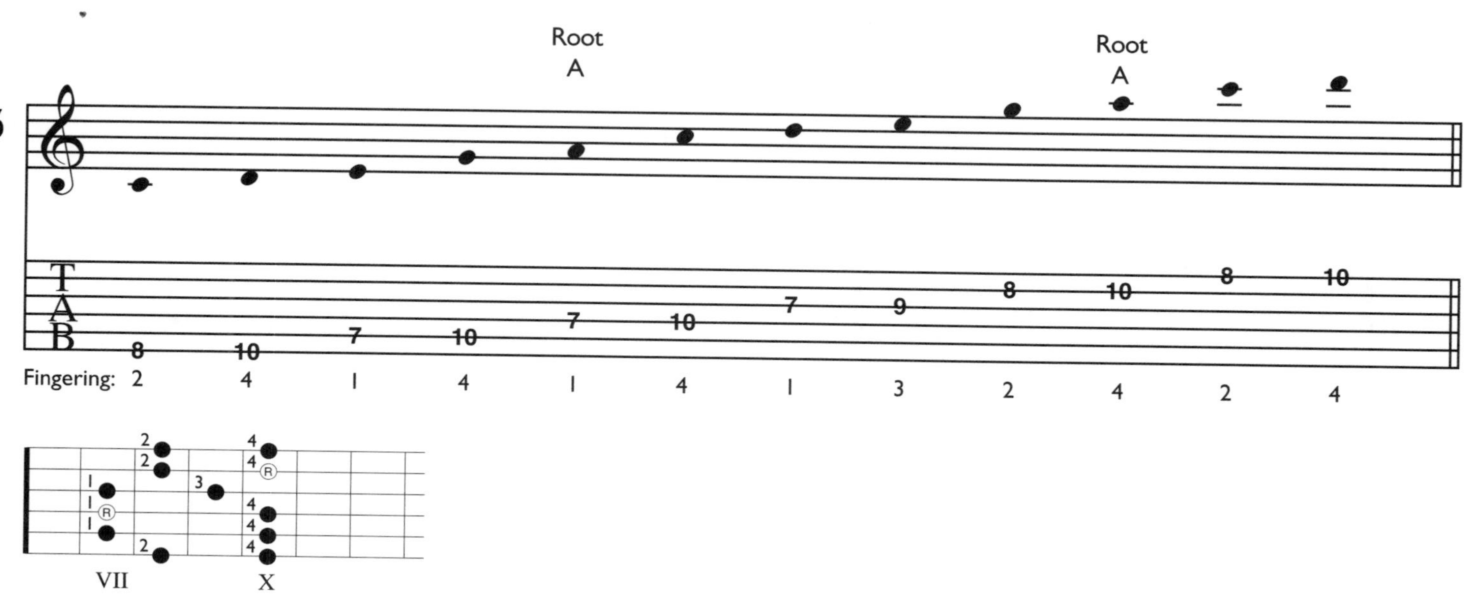

Practicing these examples will help you learn this fingering.

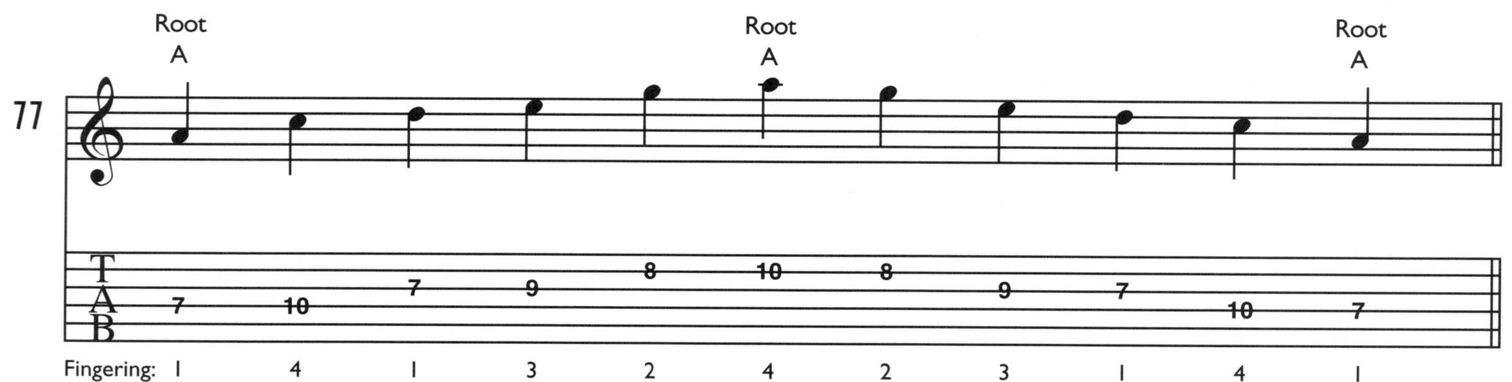

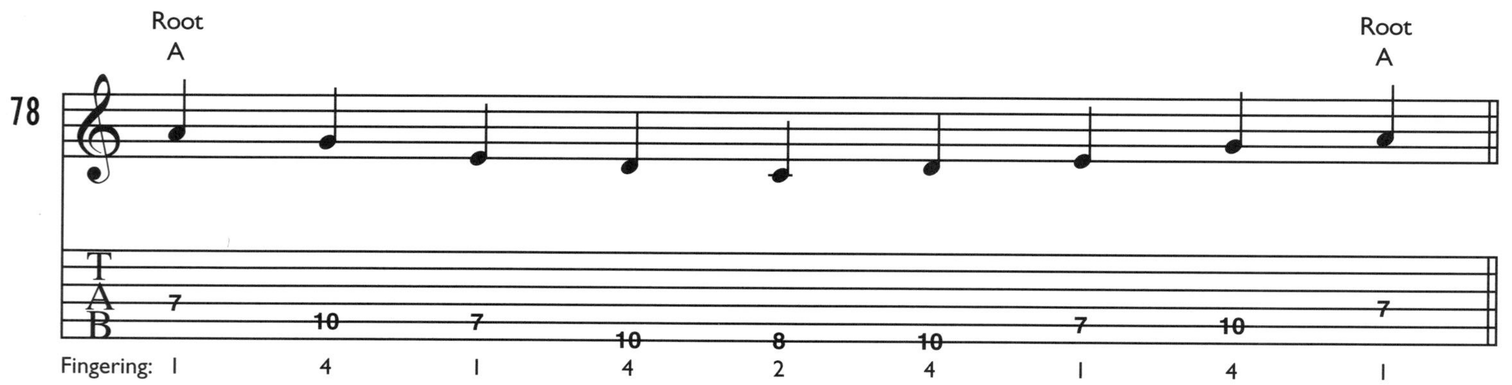

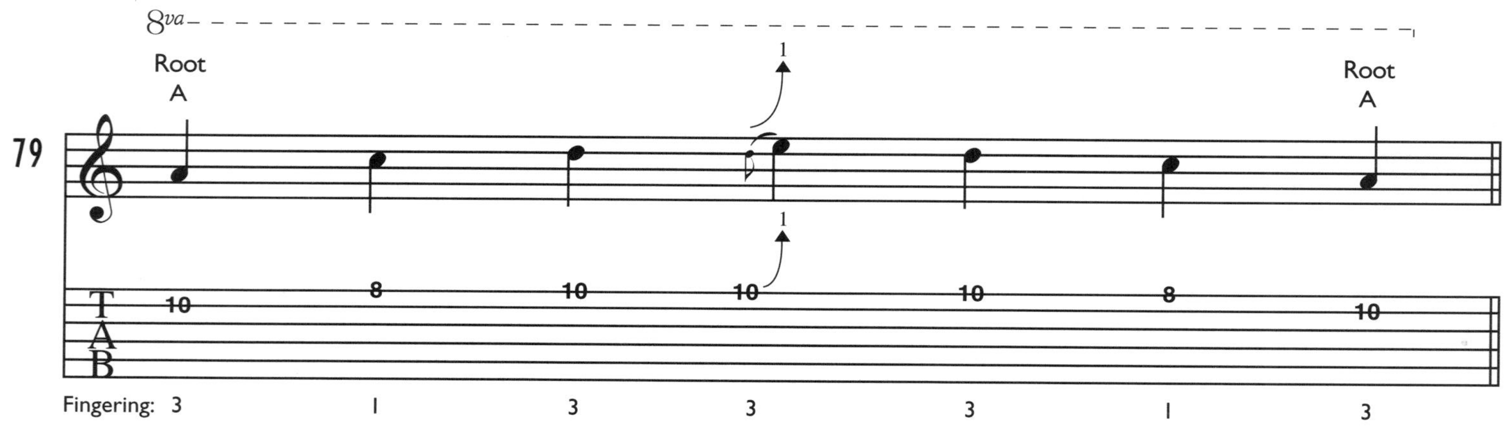

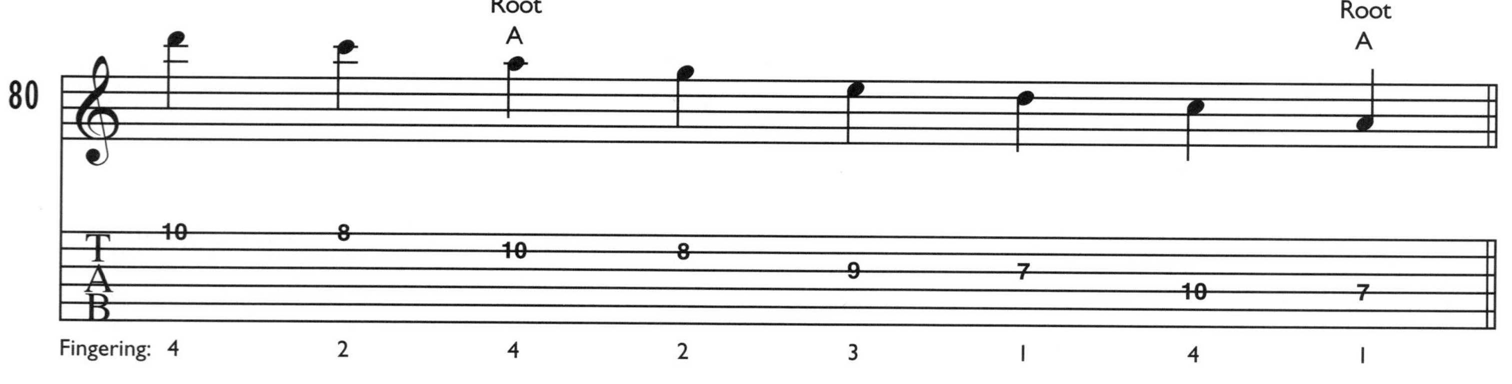

PRACTICING FINGERING #2

Practice the scale up and down as you did with Fingering #1 (see page 35). Develop as many melodic patterns and licks from the new fingering as you can. Look for places to use left-hand techniques such as bends and slides. Examples 81 through 85 will get you started. They are in the 7th position.

Remember, this is still the same five-note scale you learned back in Chapter 4. Learn every new fingering we cover in a few common keys first (such as A, E and G). Then try it in all keys and start from every possible root in the fingering. Experiment!

PHOTO • ROBERT KNIGHT

Jimi Hendrix

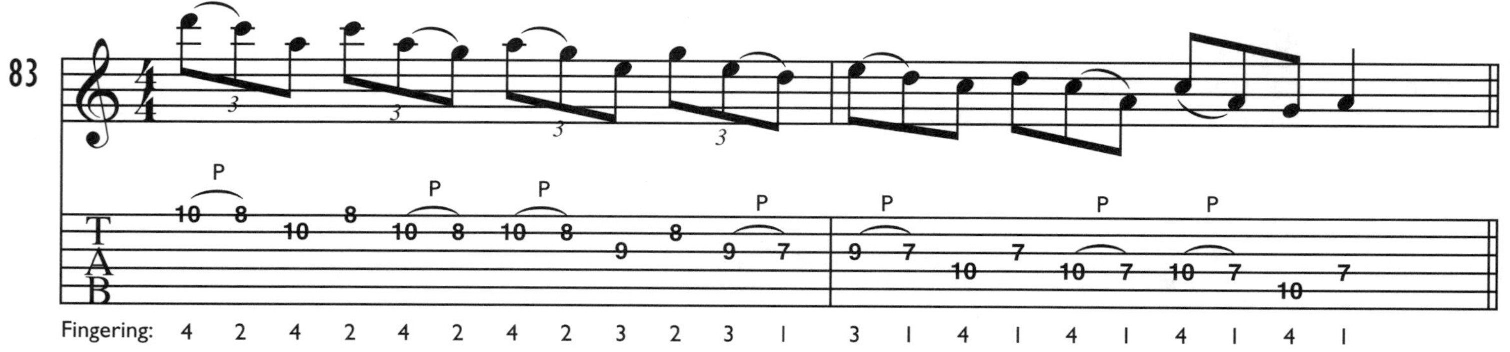
83
Fingering: 4 2 4 2 4 2 4 2 3 2 3 1 3 1 4 1 4 1 4 1 4 1

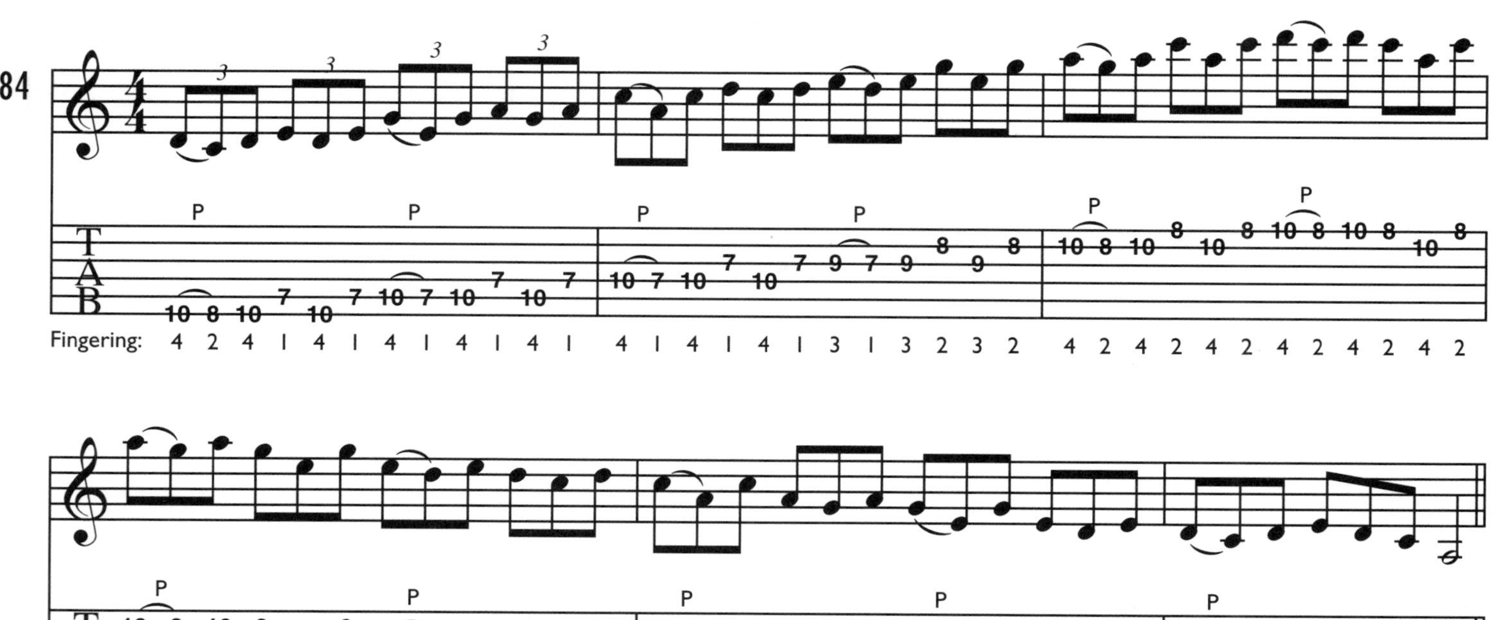
84
Fingering: 4 2 4 1 4 1 4 1 4 1 4 1 4 1 4 1 4 1 3 1 3 2 3 2 4 2 4 2 4 2 4 2 4 2 4 2
4 2 4 2 3 2 3 1 3 1 4 1 4 1 4 1 4 1 4 1 4 1 4 1 4 2 4 1 4 2 1

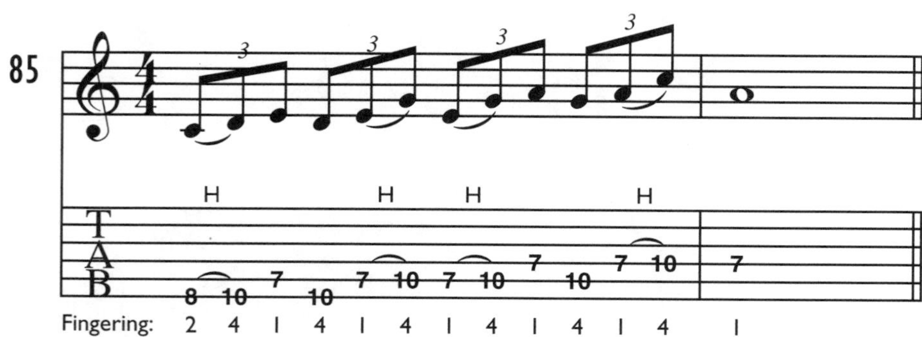
85
Fingering: 2 4 1 4 1 4 1 4 1 4 1 4 1

BENDS IN FINGERING #2

The diagrams below show the locations of the most common notes to bend in the new fingering. Practice bending in tune on half and whole step bends. Use vibrato to add life to sustained notes. Try to develop licks using appropriate bends. Work on vibrato, starting slowly and getting faster. It is important to keep pressure on the string while bending or using vibrato.

WHOLE STEP BENDS

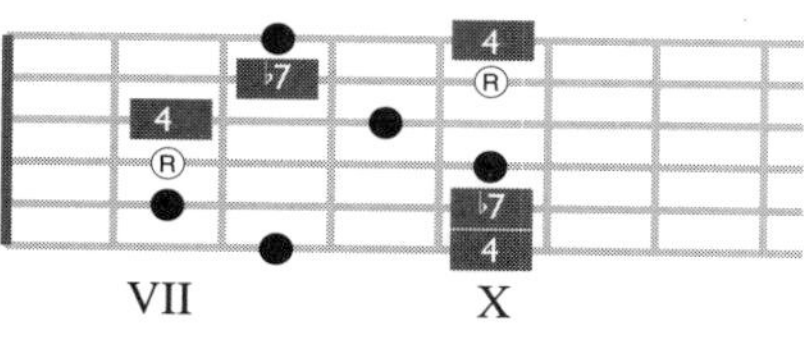

HALF STEP BENDS

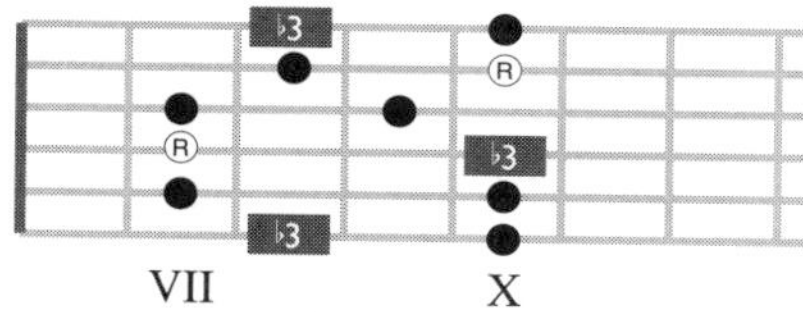

Examples 86 through 90 will give you some practice bending in Fingering #2.

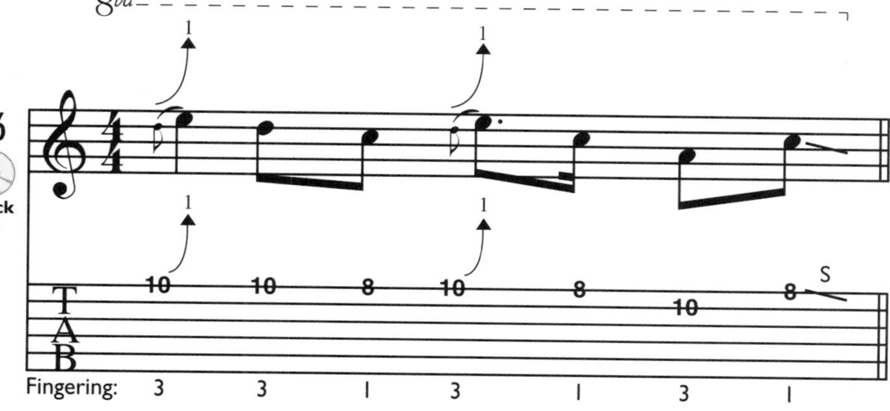

PHOTO • COURTESY OF IBANEZ

John Petrucci of Dream Theatre

Swing the eighths in Examples 87 - 90.

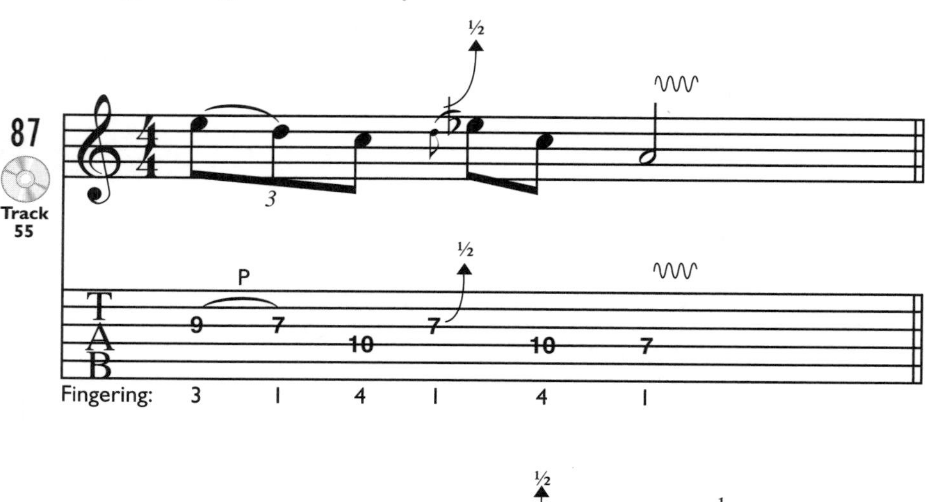

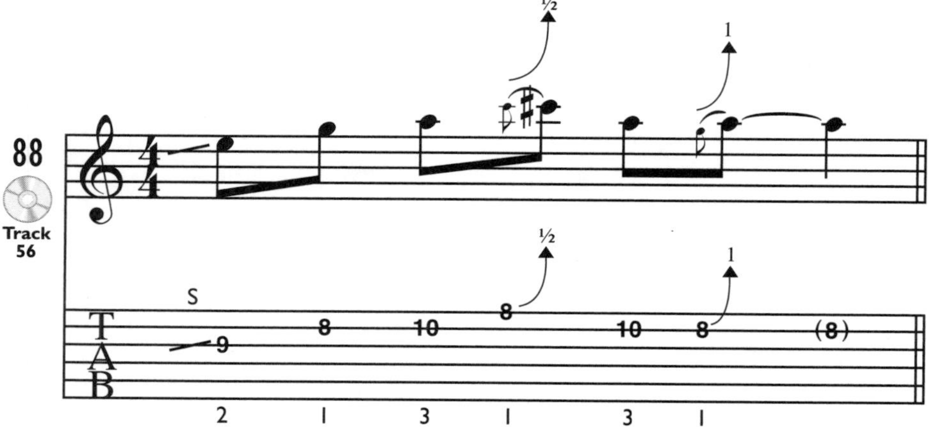

Notice the prebend in Example 89. Bend the D up to E before you play, then pluck and release the bend. See page 42 to review about this technique.

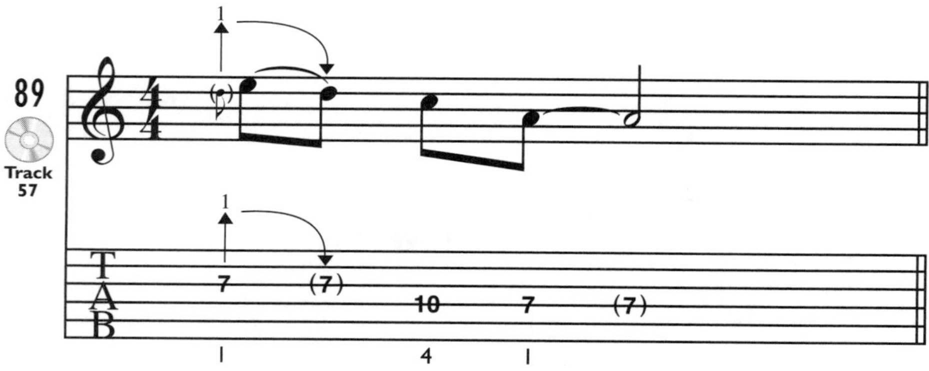

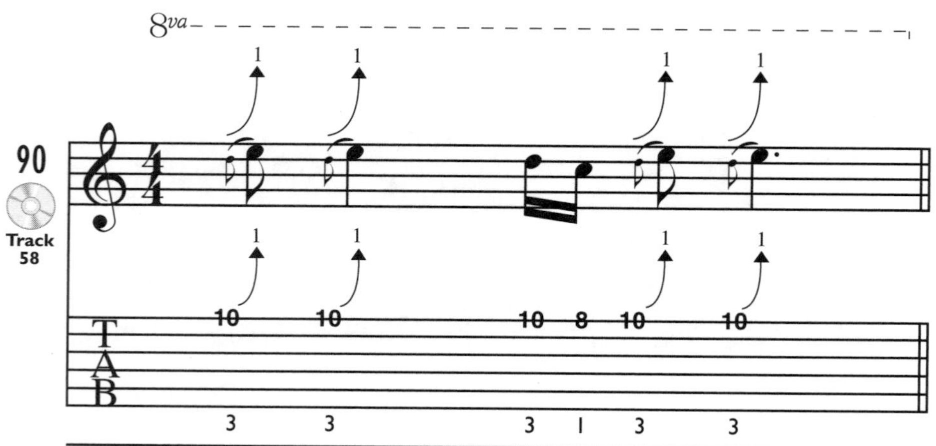

Taken together, all the fingerings of the minor pentatonic scale form a system. In order to complete the minor pentatonic system, we must learn three more box position fingerings of the scale. The diagrams on the following pages show these fingerings for the key of A with some representative licks and riffs for each. Learn to use the fingerings in all keys. Find your way by locating root notes.

When you practice soloing with the new fingerings, play over appropriate progressions in different keys. For instance, try Chapter 4, Examples 34 through 36 (page 34). Try to limit yourself to soloing with just the new fingering for a while. Try to find the notes that you want to hear within each new area of the neck. Try riffs that you know in one fingering in other fingerings.

A good method for developing solo ideas is to start by limiting yourself to a few notes. Create ideas using these few notes (see Example 97D). You will be surprised at the variations you can come up with. Vary the order and rhythms of the notes. Try to come up with ideas that sound resolved or complete. Proceed to using more notes of the scale for your ideas.

MINOR PENTATONIC SCALE FINGERING #3

91

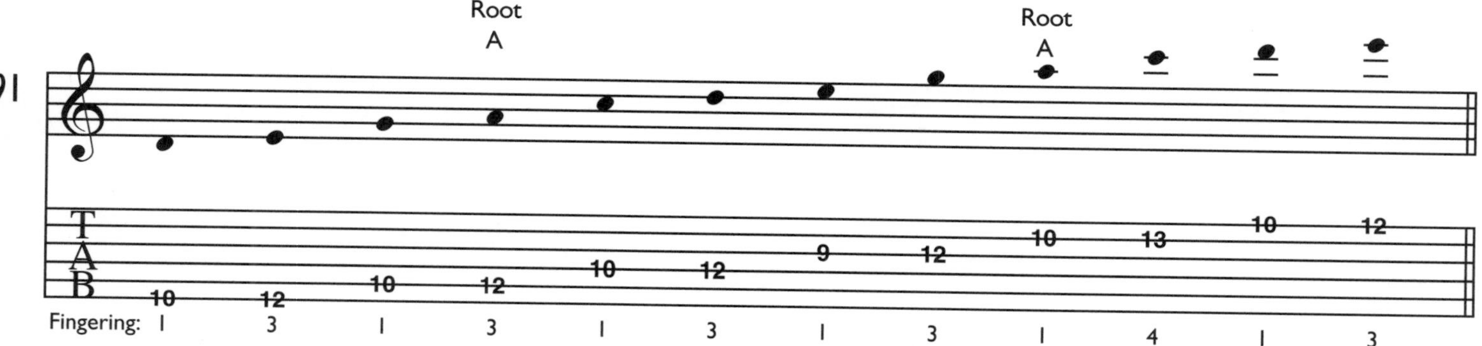

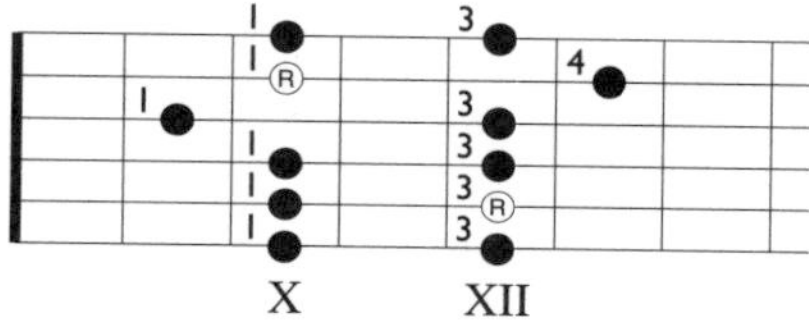

Swing the eighths in Example 92.

92

Track 59

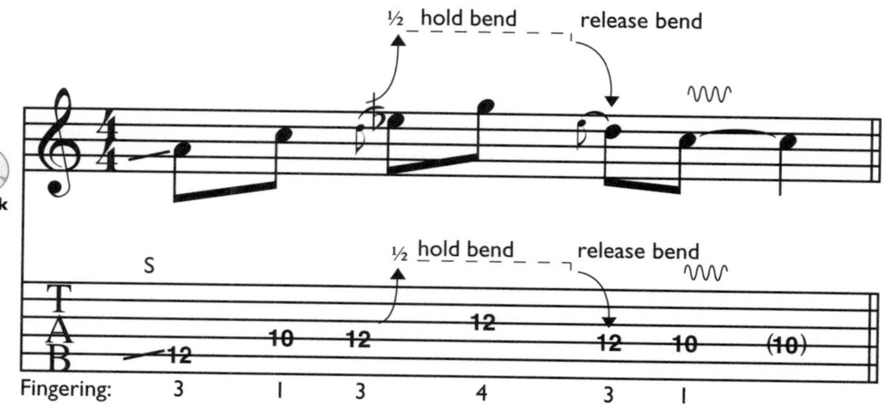

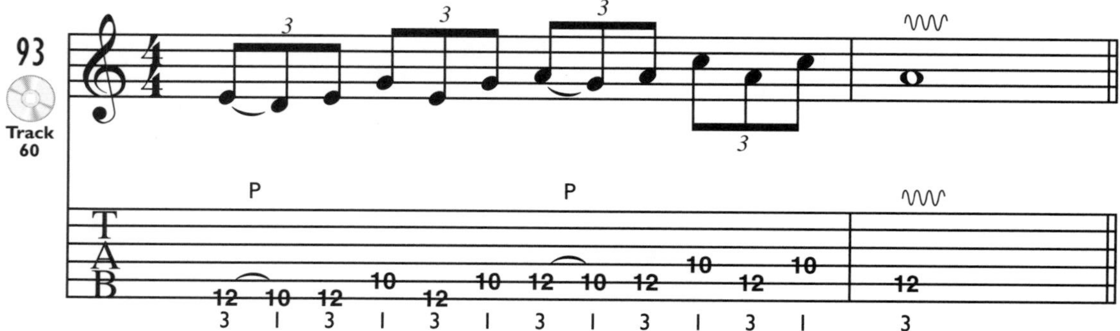

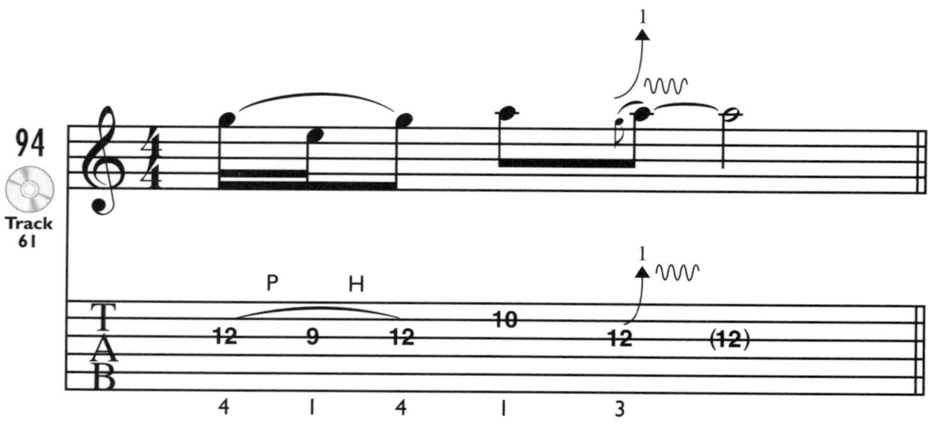

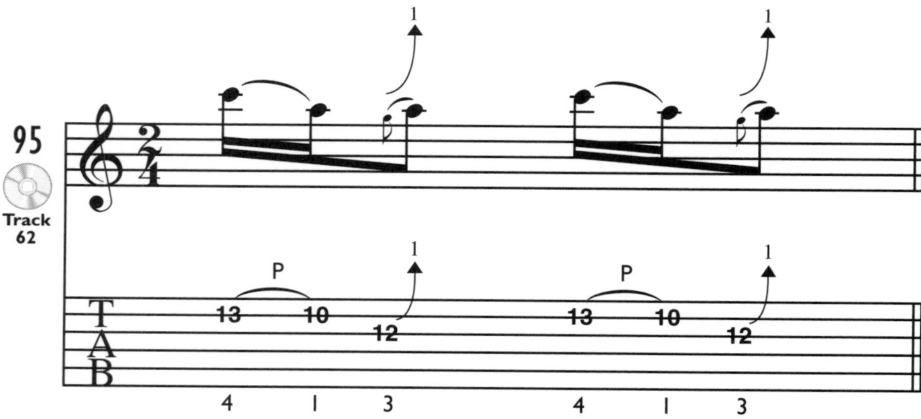

Remember that the best notes to bend are 4 to ♭5 or ♮5 and ♭3 to ♮3 or 4. Look for slurs (hammer-ons, pull-offs and slides) that lie comfortably in each fingering. Also, learn to play each fingering from top to bottom and vice-versa, using alternate picking for speed and clarity. Always start slowly and build up speed gradually.

MINOR PENTATONIC SCALE FINGERING #4

96

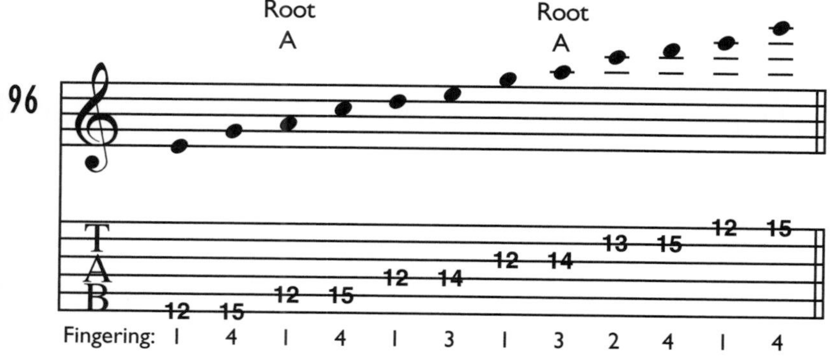

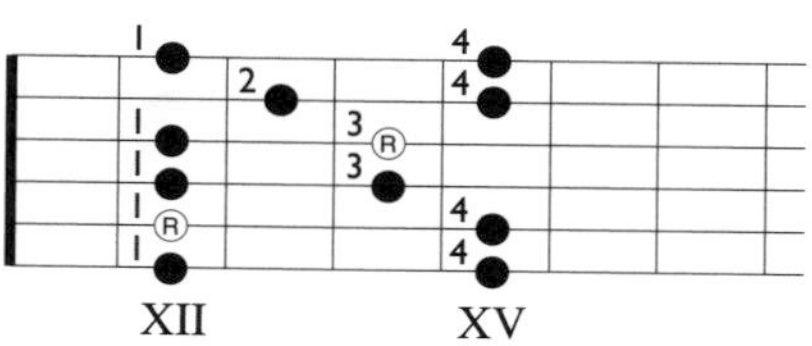

Swing the eighths in Example 97.

97

Track 63

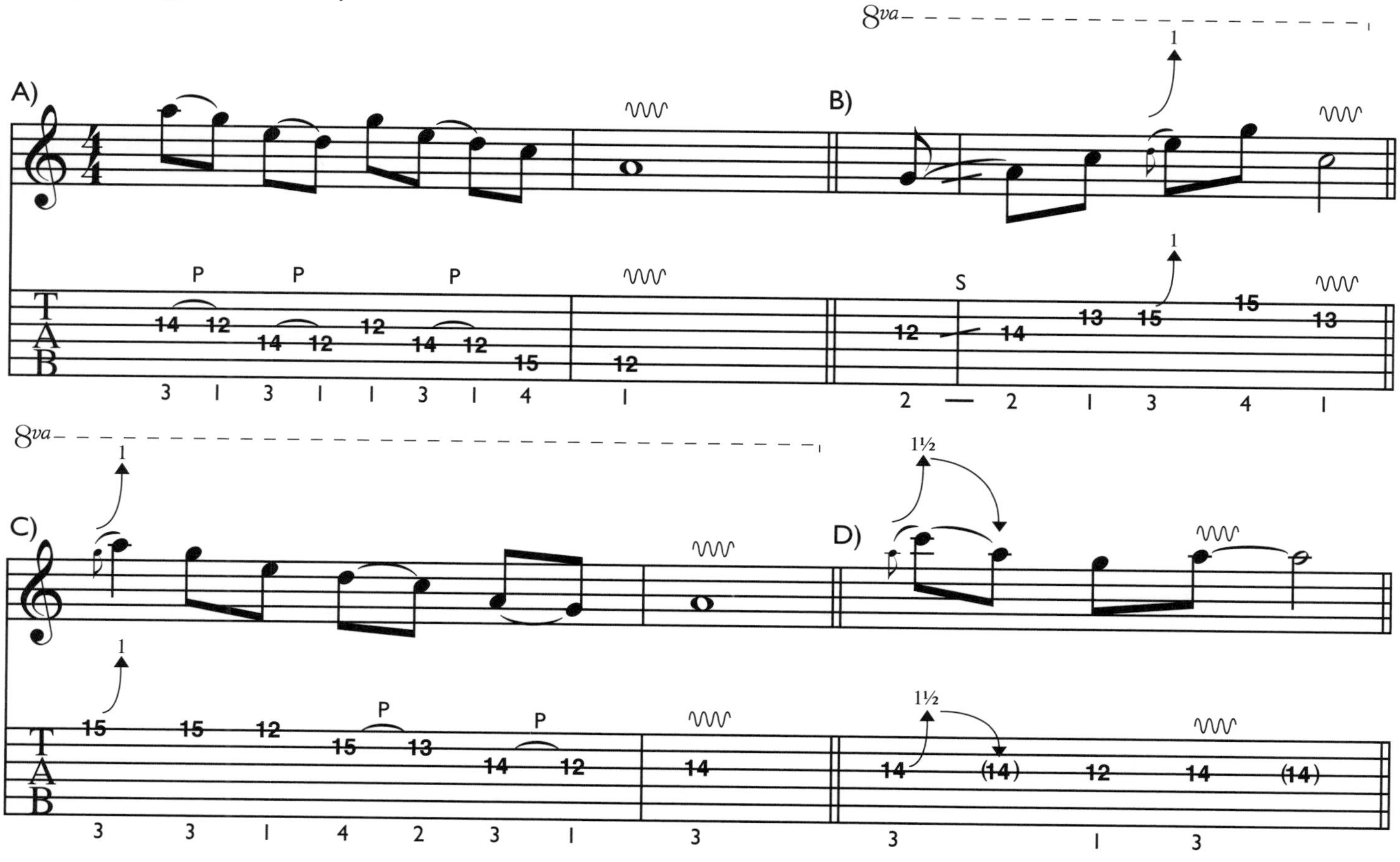

A)

B)

C)

D)

It is a good idea to return to the root note every so often to reinforce the key in your ear.

MINOR PENTATONIC SCALE FINGERING #5

98

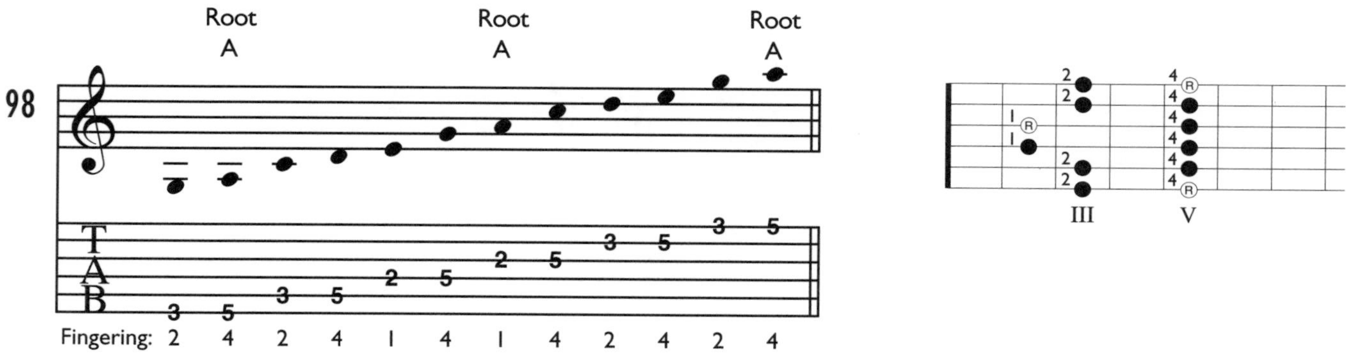

Example 99A sounds best with swing eighths, but play 99C with straight eighths.

99

MINOR PENTATONIC CONNECTIONS

Besides learning the static box position fingerings of the minor pentatonic scale, you need to learn connecting routes from fingering to fingering. We do this by utilizing sliding licks that bring us up or down the neck. The examples that follow show sliding patterns that allow us to play the minor pentatonic scale in this more linear fashion. Refer also to the E Minor Pentatonic sliding scale in Chapter 4. The brackets in the standard notation show which fingerings are being connected.

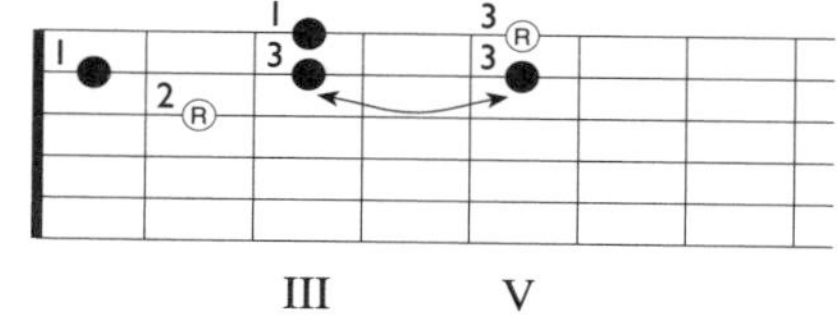

#5 - - - - = Notes with this bracket are from Fingering #5

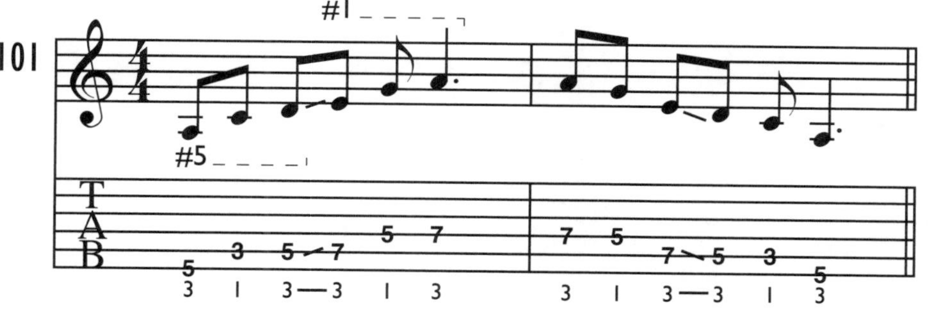

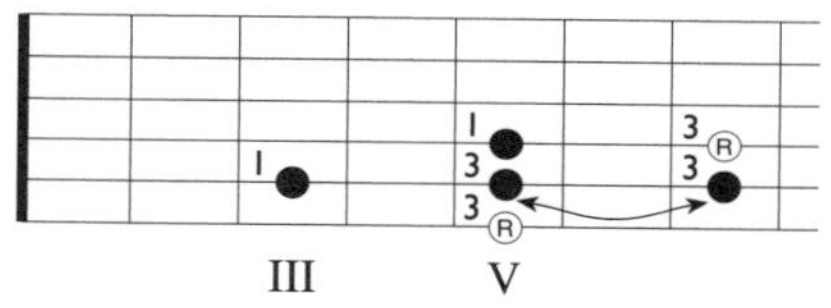

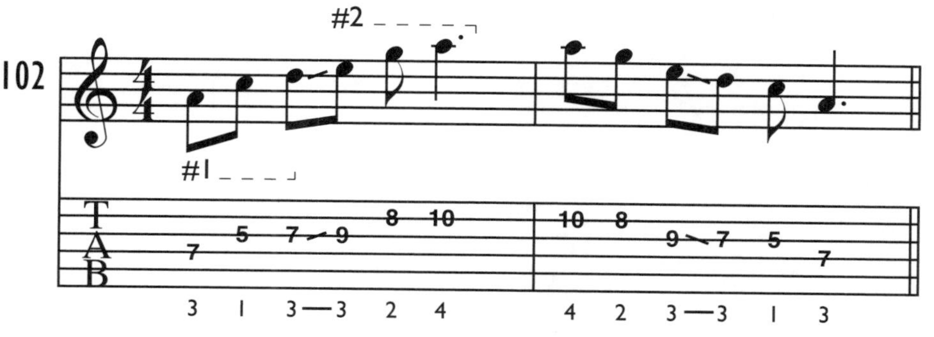

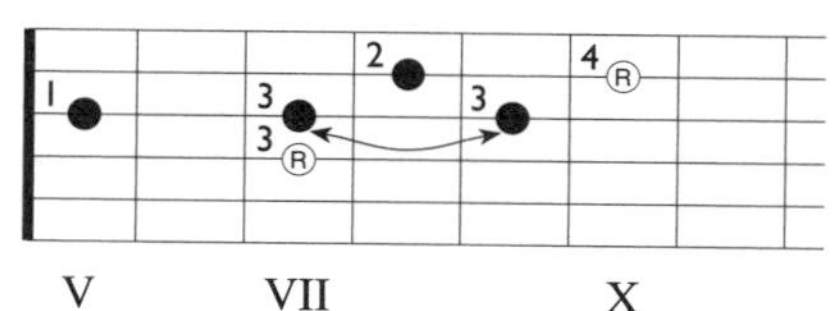

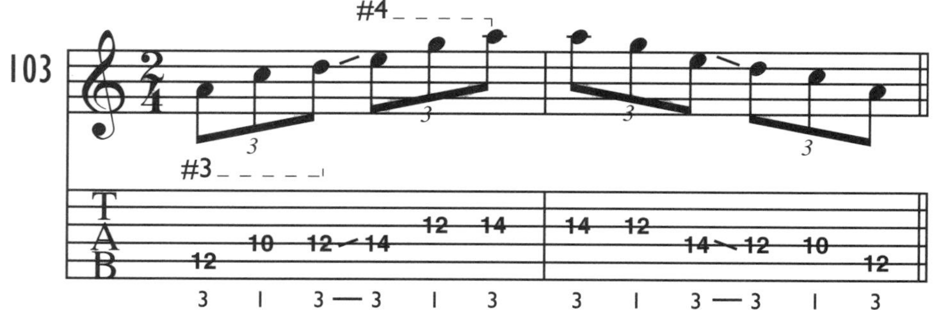

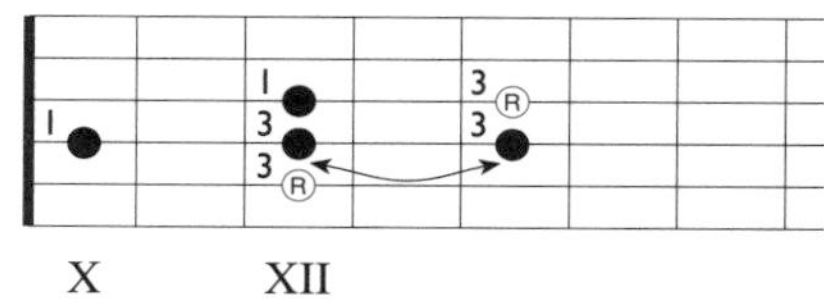

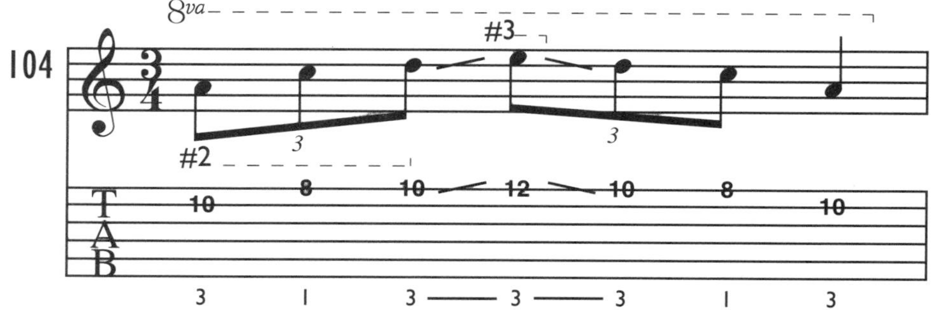

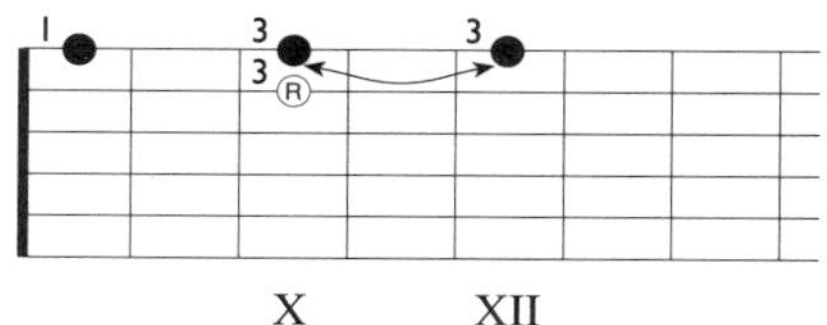

PHOTO • TERRY O'NEILL/COURTESY OF REPRISE RECORDS

Eric Clapton

105
#2
#1
T
A
B
5 8 10 7 10 7 7 10 7 10 8 5
1 4 4 1 4 1 1 4 1 4 4 1

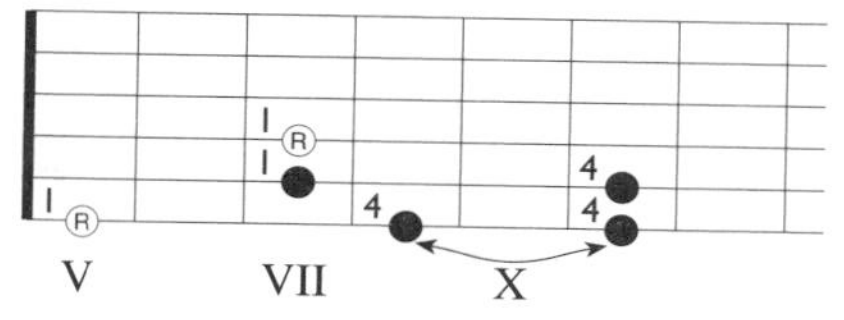
V
VII
X

106
#3
#2
T
A
B
7 10 12 9 12 10 10 12 9 12 10 7
1 4 4 1 4 2 2 4 1 4 4 1

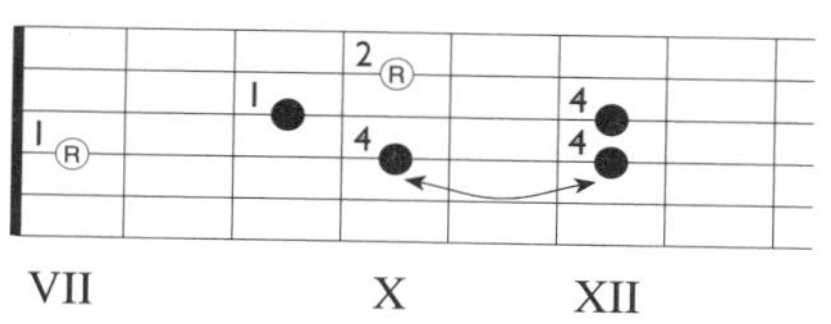
VII
X
XII

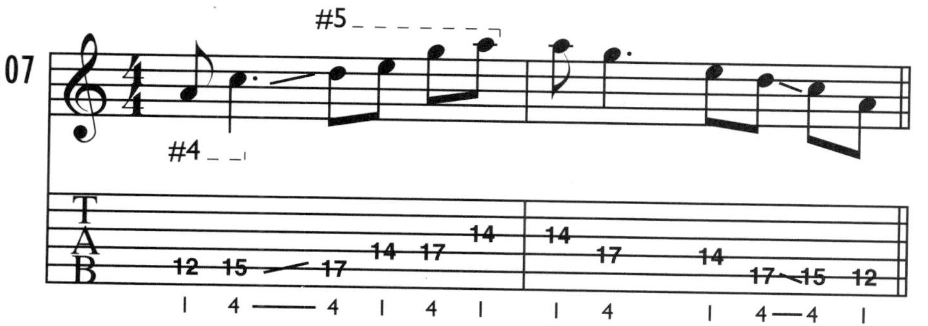
107
#5
#4
T
A
B
12 15 17 14 17 14 14 17 14 17 15 12
1 4 4 1 4 1 1 4 1 4 4 1

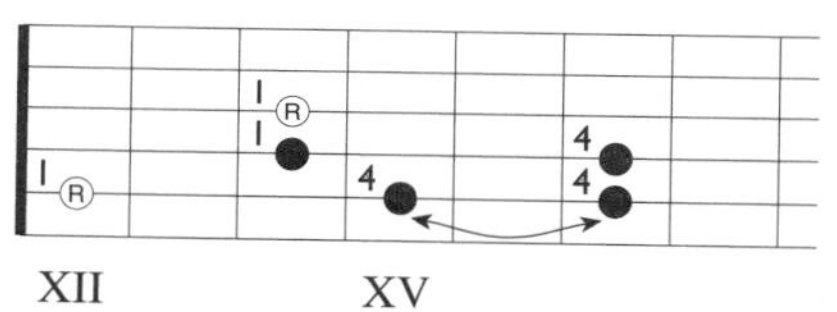
XII
XV

THE ENTIRE MINOR PENTATONIC SYSTEM

THE FORMULA

1 ♭3 4 5 ♭7

THE FINGERINGS AND THEIR CONNECTIONS IN THE KEY OF A

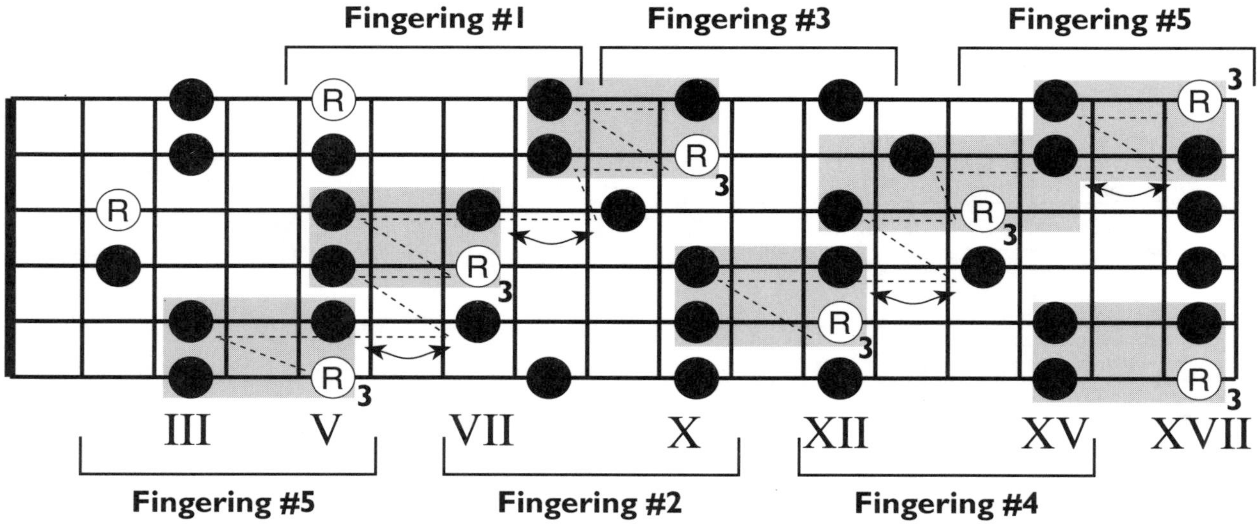

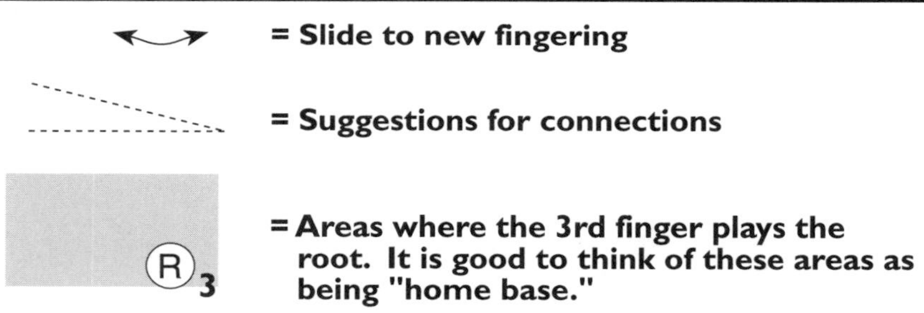

CHAPTER 8

The Blues

When the African musical traditions of the slaves met up with the western instruments and musical traditions of colonial America, the blues was born. All rock, pop and jazz music owes a huge debt to its blues roots.

One of the characteristic sounds of the blues is the use of flatted or *blue notes* over major chords. Our ears are so used to this sound that it now seems perfectly natural. The use of blue notes (♭3, ♭5 and ♭7), even though the chords may have ♮3 and ♮5 tones, is the essence of the blues sound. Emotional content is also extremely important.

THE TWELVE-BAR BLUES

The word *blues* conjures up not only a sound image but a form as well. The basic blues form is called the *twelve-bar blues*. This form is a chord progression that is twelve measures (bars) in length and uses a particular sequence of the I, IV and V chords. In a blues the chords are often all dominant 7th chords. Use the A Minor Pentatonic scale to improvise throughout Example 108, but be sensitive about how your note choices sound over the chords—try to *resolve* (come to rest) to notes that belong to the chords.

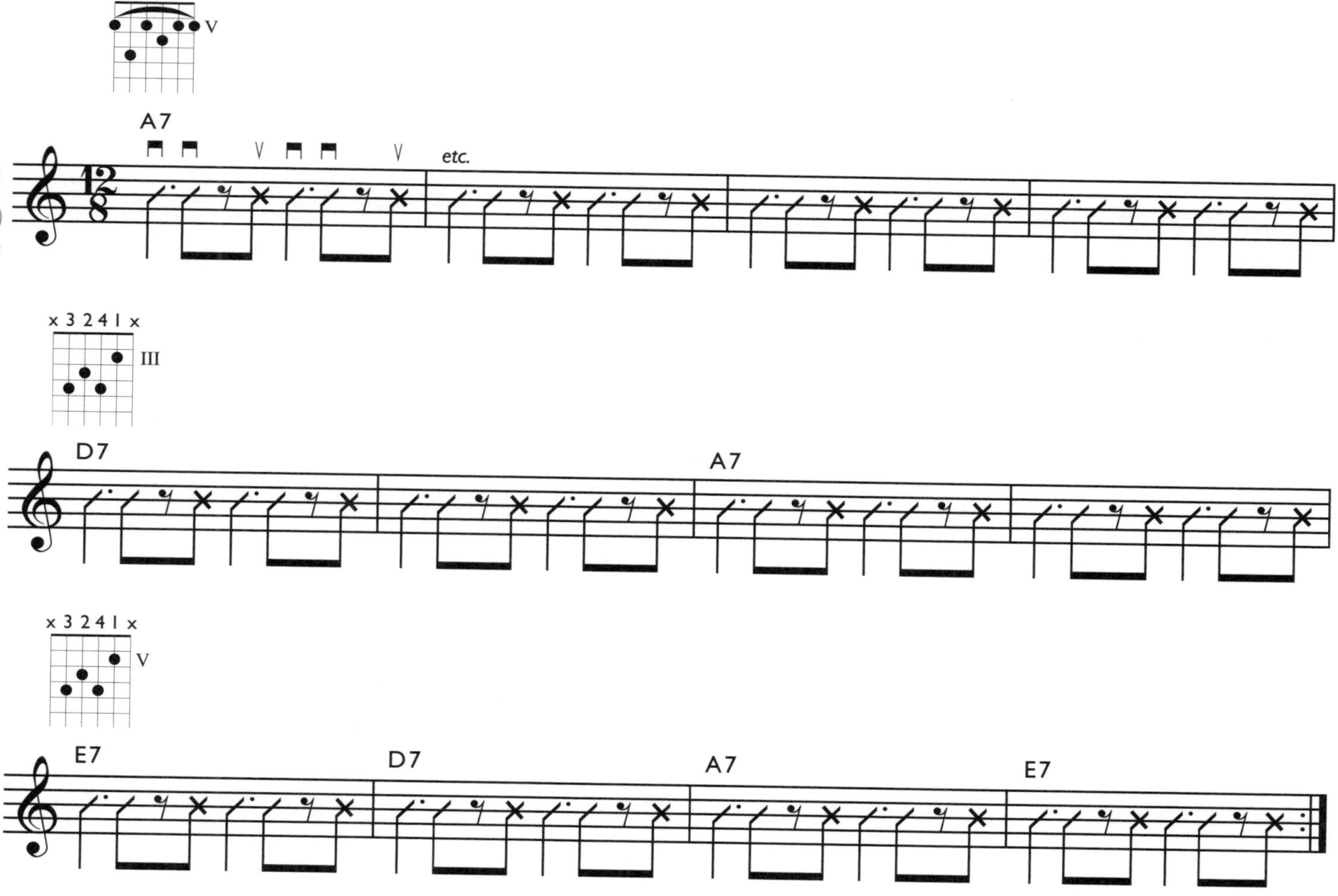

Here is a sample solo for the blues chord progression in Example 108. Notice that some of the notes are bent only a quarter-tone (¼). This means the note is bent only a very slight amount. The result is a note "in the crack," halfway between the note and its neighbor one half step above.

OPEN STRING SHUFFLE AND RHYTHM RIFFS

Certain playing positions are very useful because of the guitar's open strings. Some are very useful for playing rhythm & blues, or shuffle style rhythm riffs in E, A and D. Notice that these keys have the same names as the lowest three strings of the guitar. By using these open strings with added chord and scale tones on adjacent strings, we can play riffs and rhythm patterns that have been the basis for hundreds of rock songs. The diagrams on the right show the three basic shuffle positions.

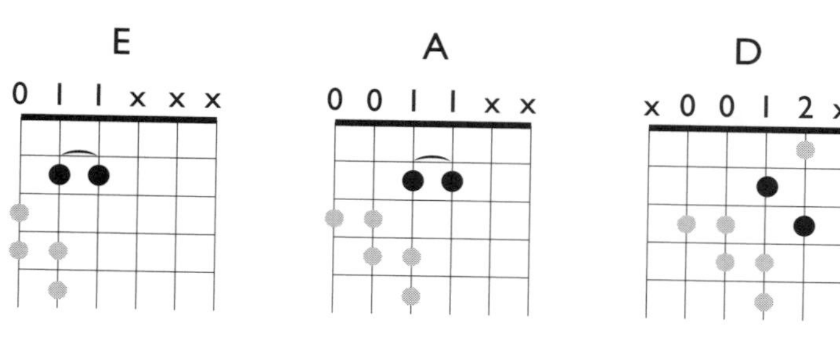

● = added scale tones

In the style of Johnny Winter

110

Track 67

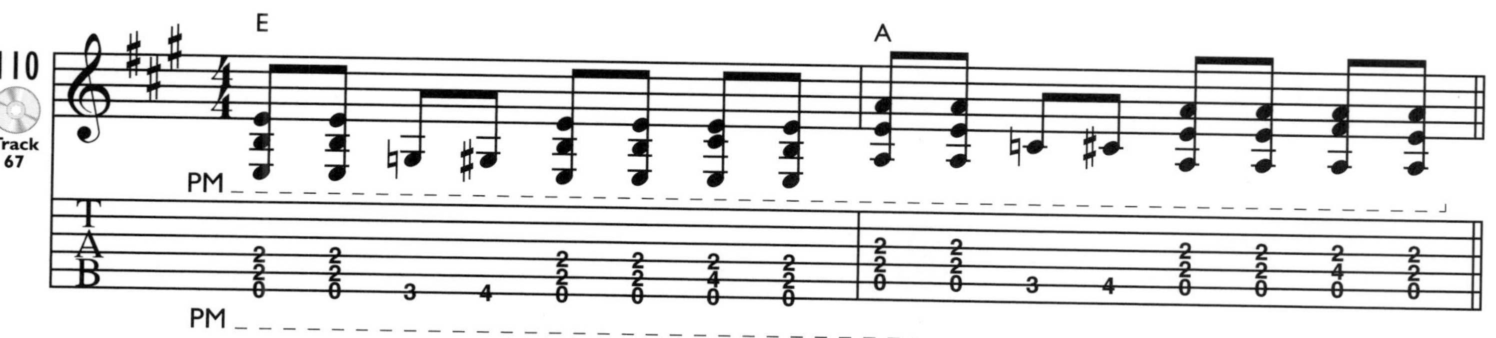

In the style of Led Zeppelin

111

Track 68

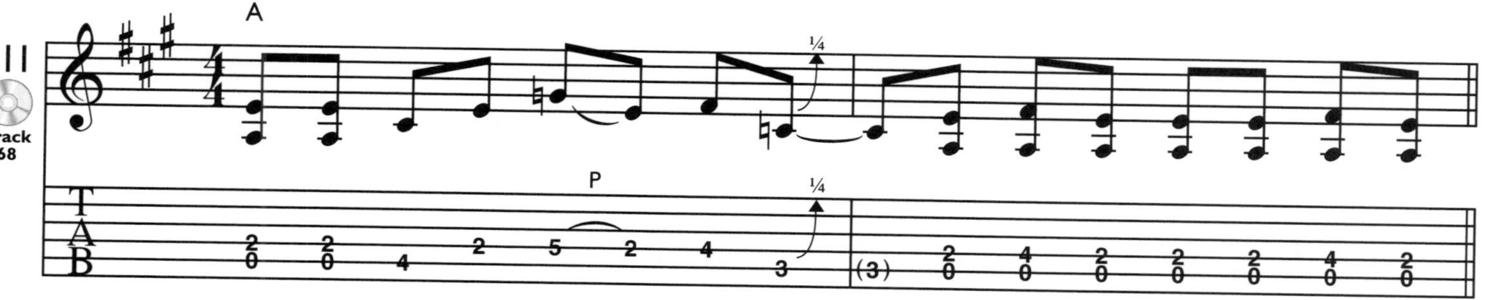

In the style of Van Halen

112

Track 69

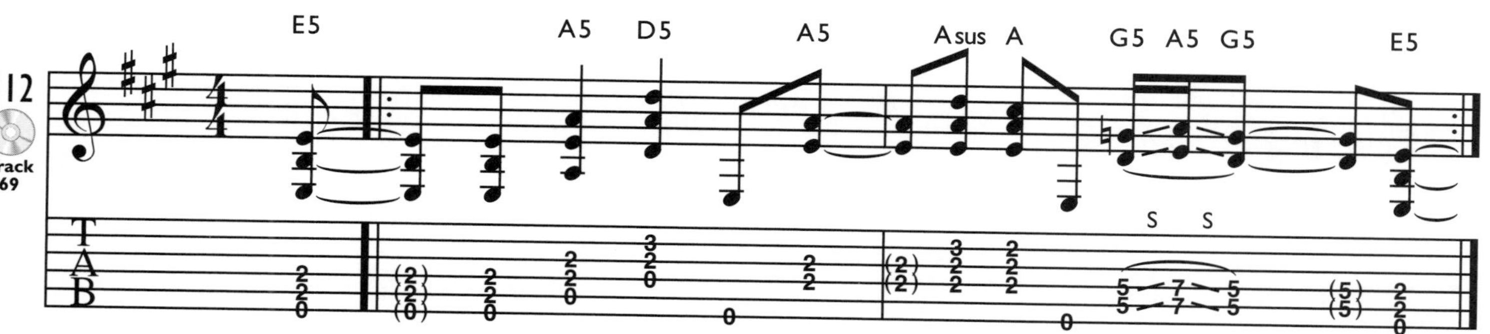

Here is an easy blues shuffle. Be sure to swing the eighths in this one! You can also try using a slight palm mute.

TWELVE-BAR BLUES IN E

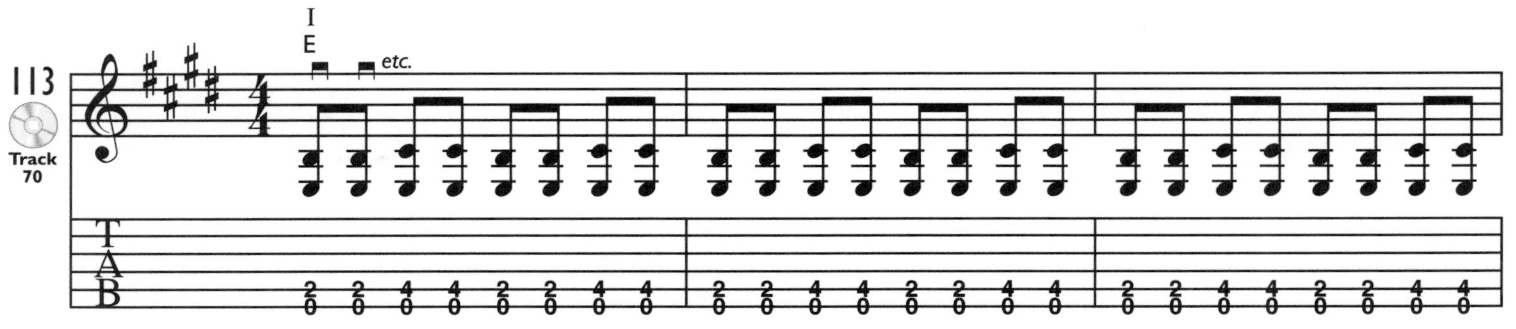

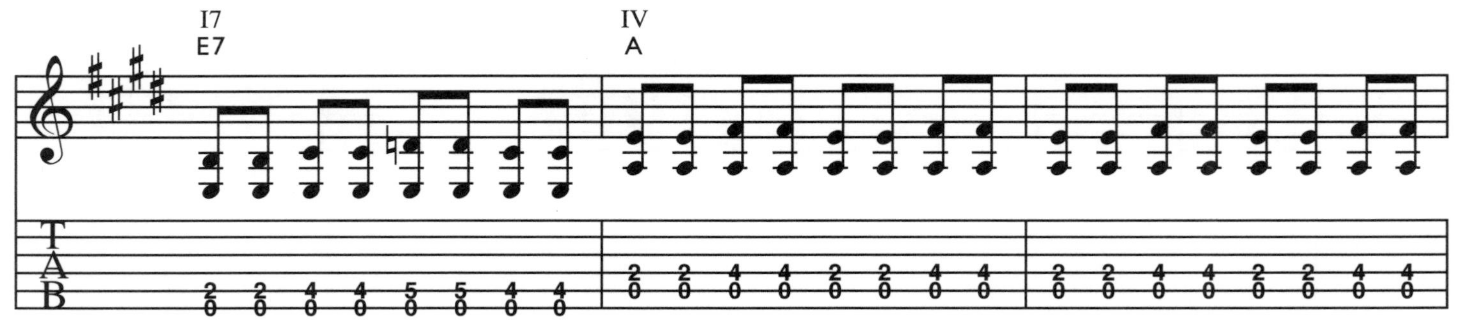

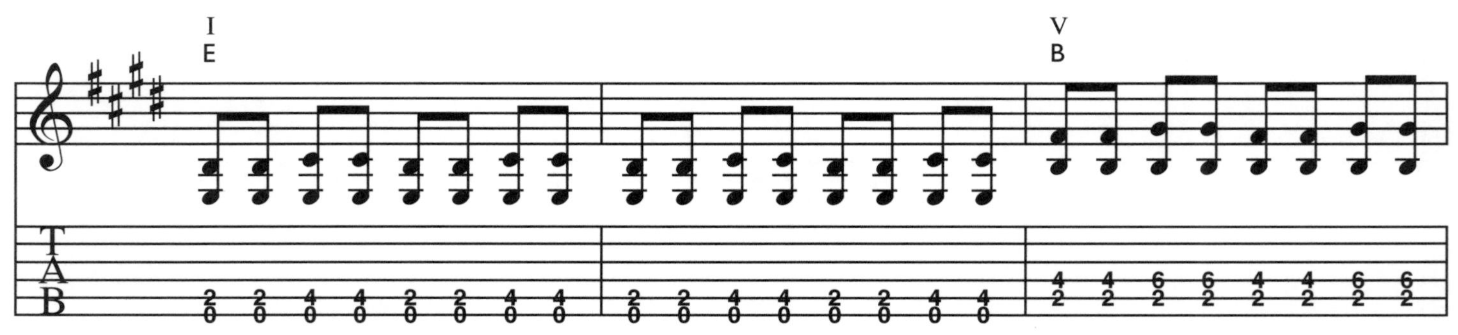

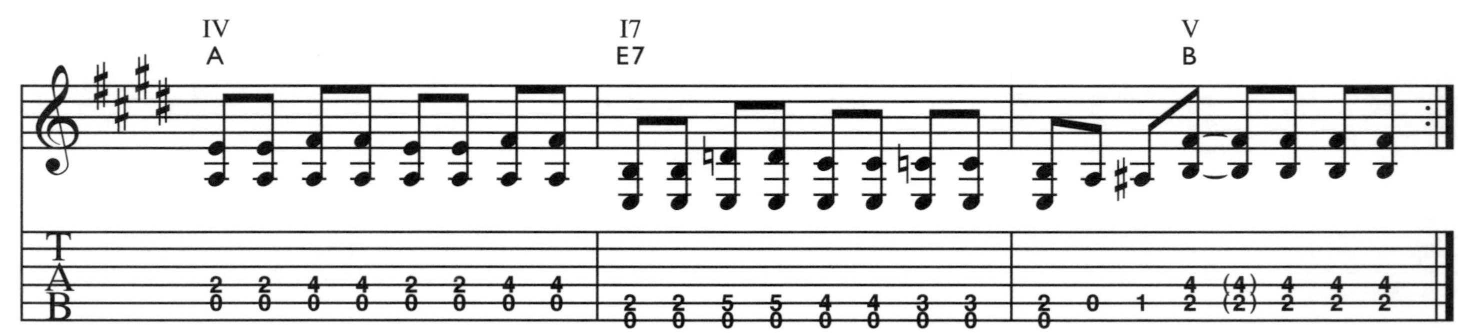

There are many possible variations on the basic blues shuffle. To use open strings you have to stay in the keys of E or A. Try using palm muting (see Chapter 3). Remember to keep your hand close to the bridge so that a good tone is produced. Use a crisp attack by striking the strings firmly. Swing the eighths!

EMBELLISHED BLUES SHUFFLE

114

Track 71

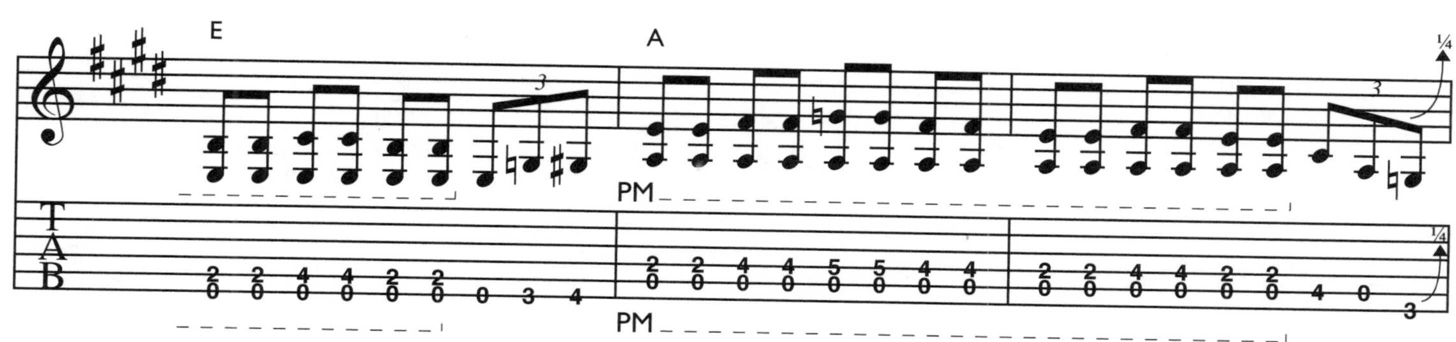

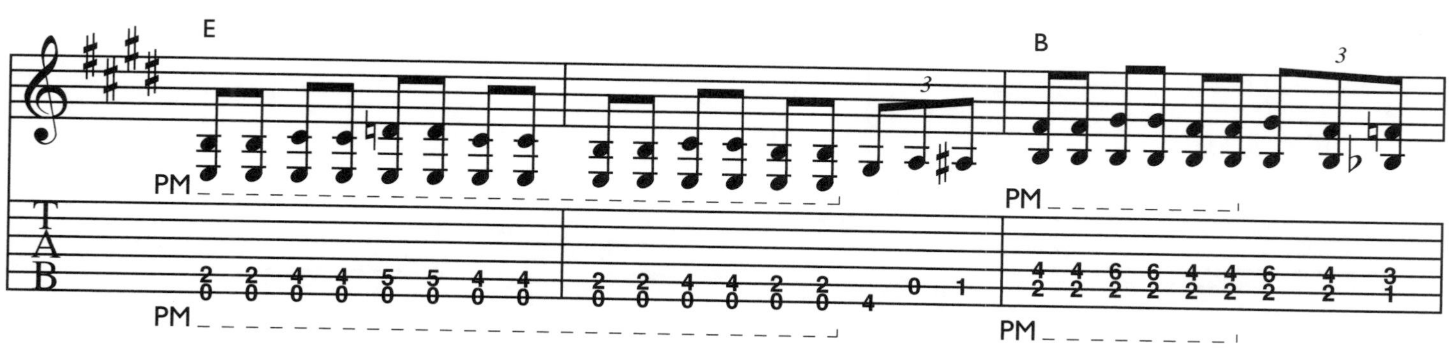

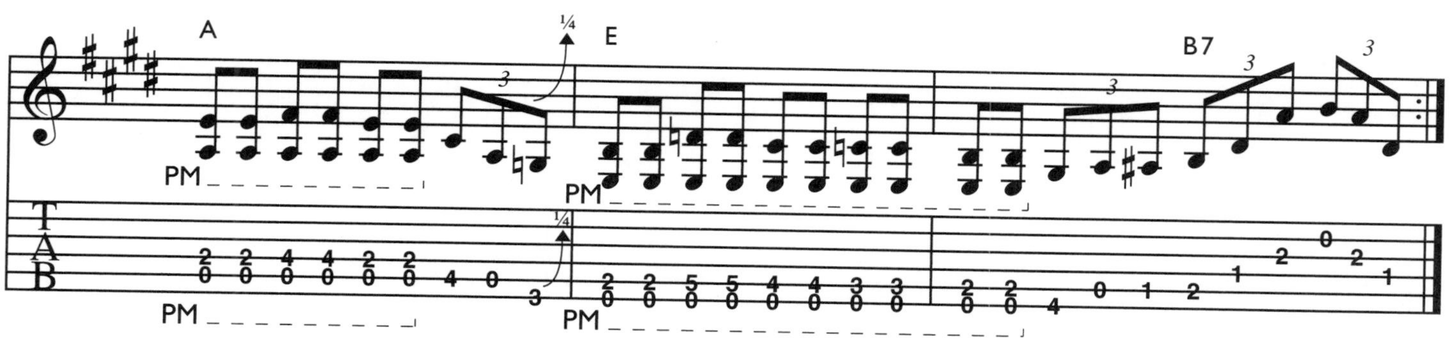

Remember, "shuffle" means to swing the eighths.

EIGHT-BAR BLUES SHUFFLE

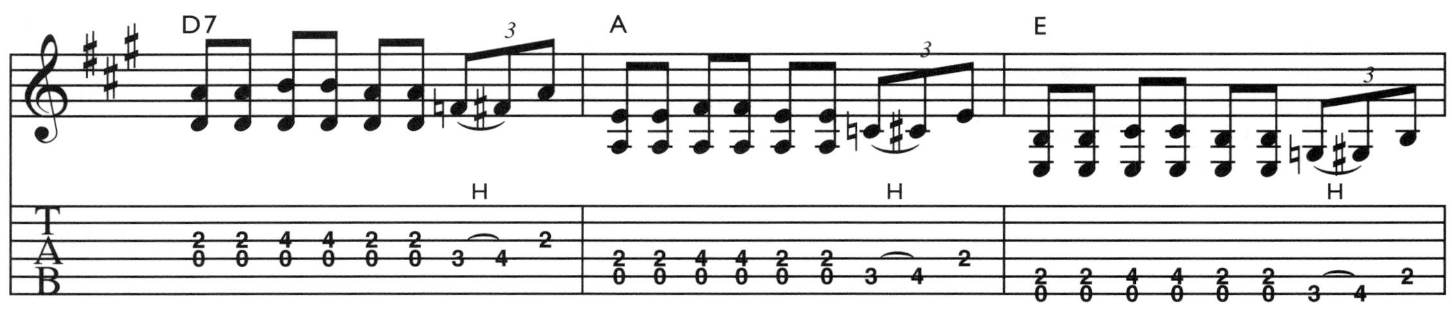

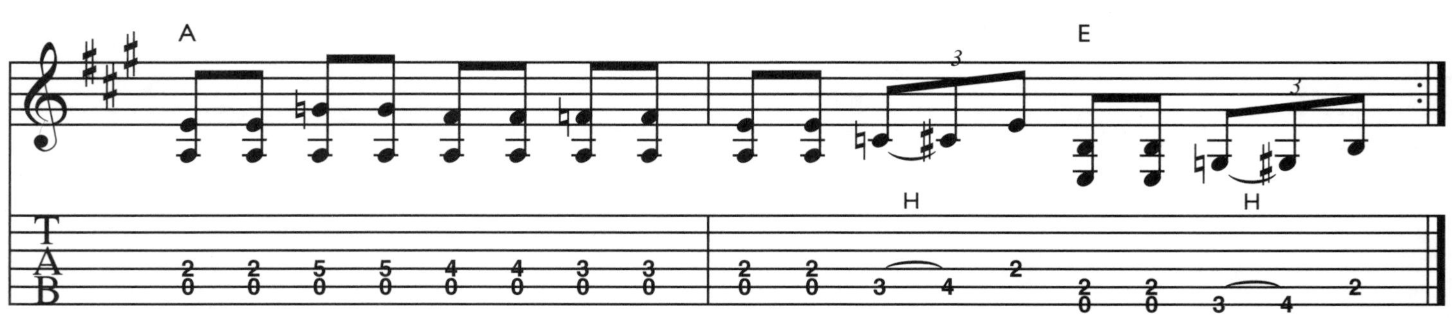

BLUES SCALES

The $^\flat$5 is frequently added to the minor pentatonic scale. The addition of this note creates the *blues scale*. Notice that the $^\flat$5 creates lots of tension—it leads us strongly to another note, usually down to the 4 or up to the $^\natural$5. The diagrams on the right show two common fingerings for the blues scale.

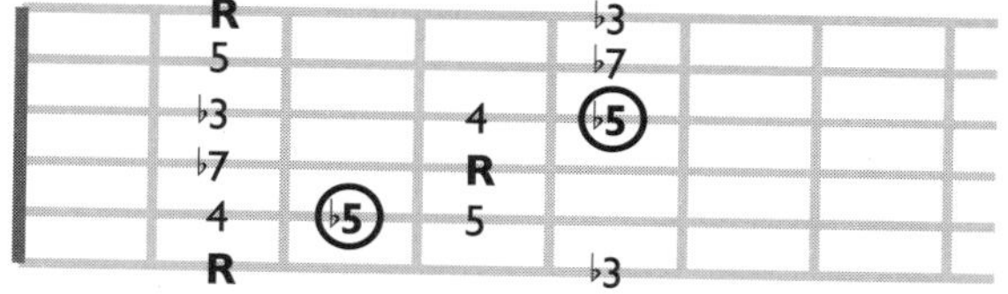

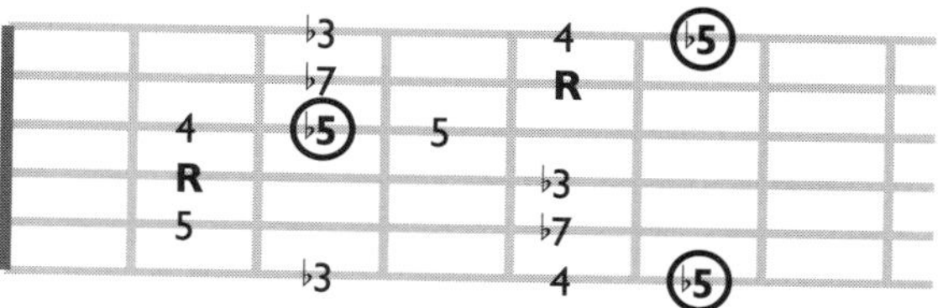

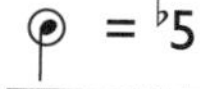

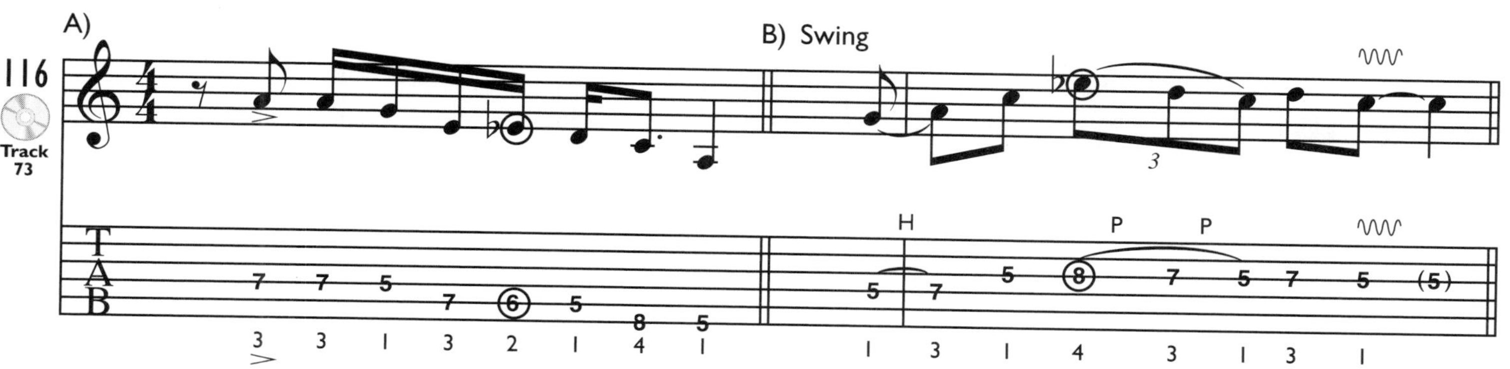

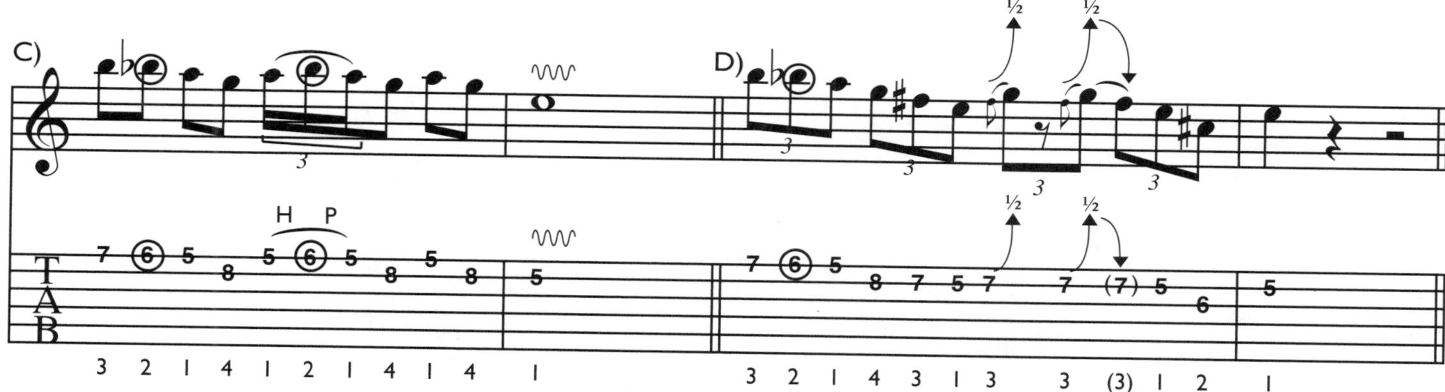

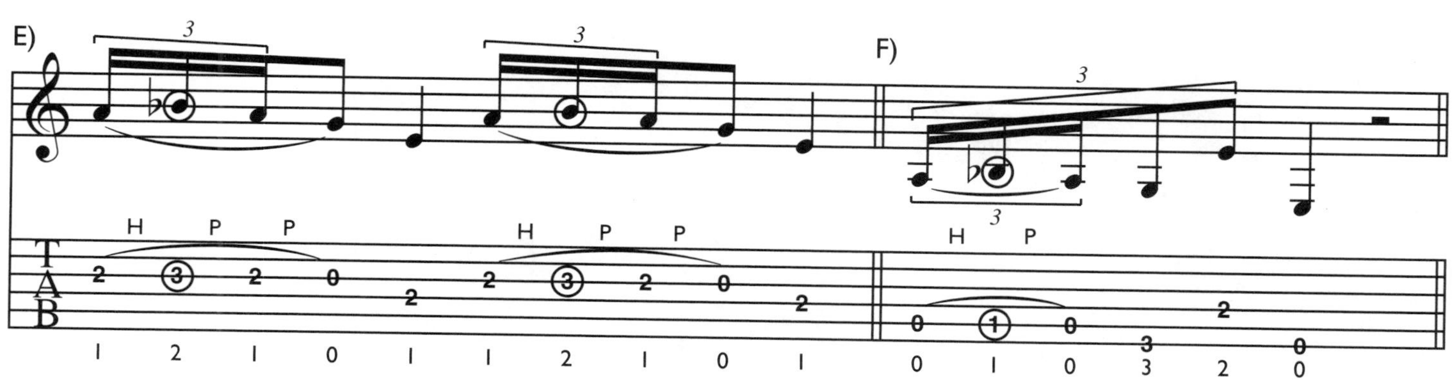

THE ENTIRE BLUES SCALE SYSTEM

THE FORMULA

1 ♭3 4 ♭5 ♮5 ♭7

THE FINGERINGS IN THE KEY OF F

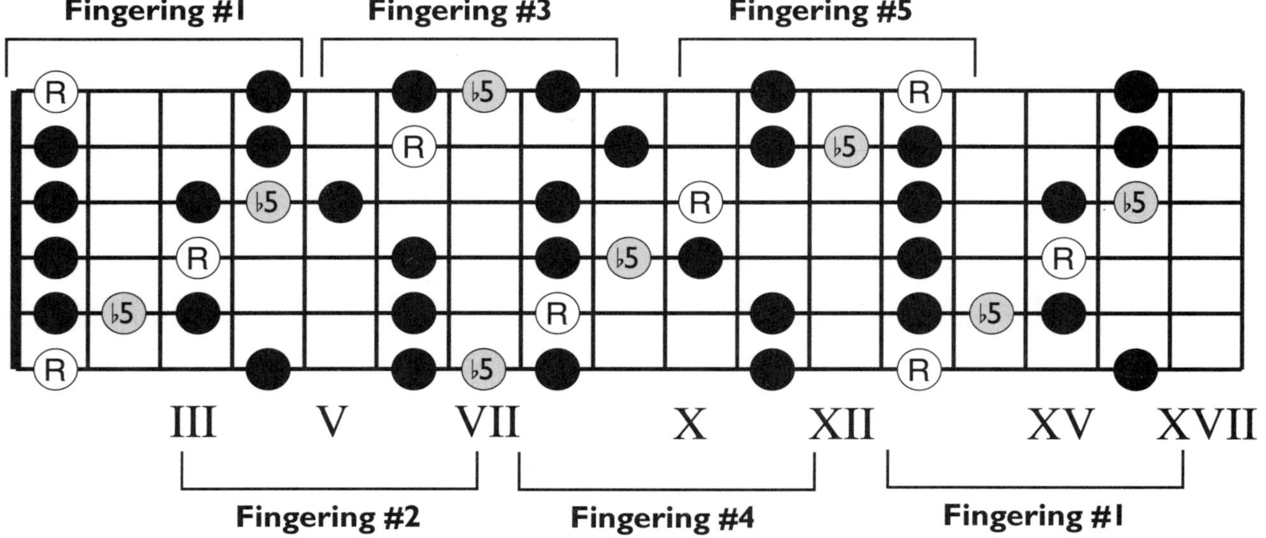

PHOTO • ROBERT KNIGHT

B. B. King

To improvise over Example 117, use the E Minor Pentatonic or blues scale. Try adding the ♮3 (G♯) over the E chord (I).

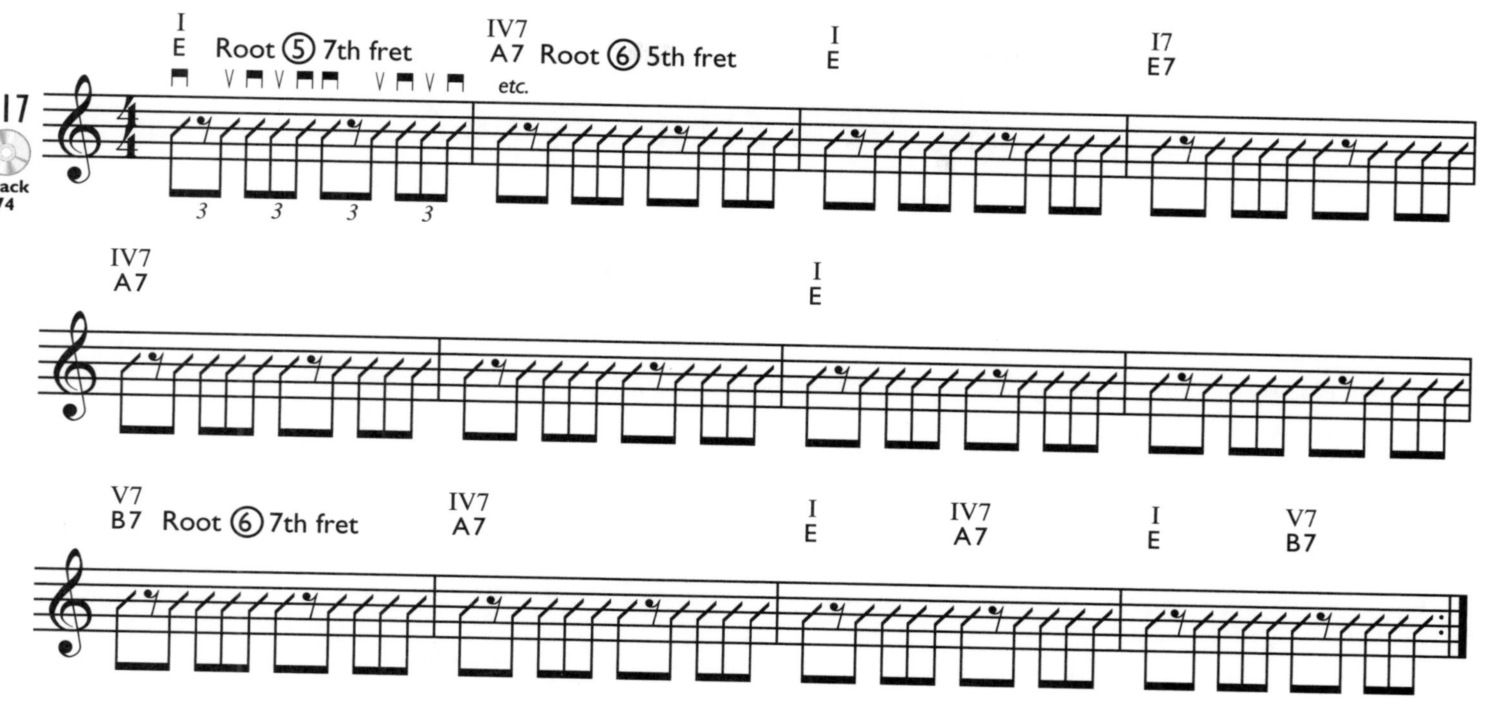

Example 118 is an eight-bar blues. Notice the dominant 7th chords on VI (E7) and II (A7). While this progression is in G, and diatonic harmony would call for a minor vi (Emin) and ii (Amin), the dominant 7th sound can show up anywhere! This is the blues!

Swing those eighths!

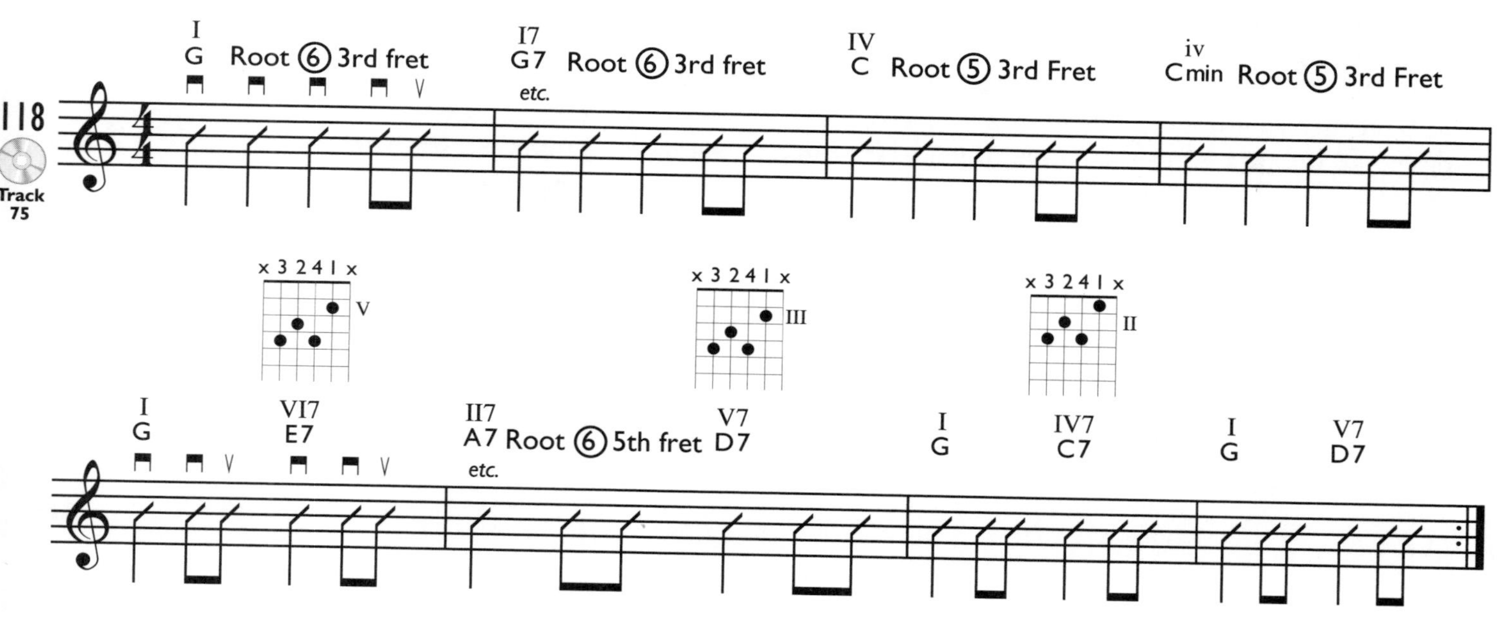

CHAPTER 9

The Major Pentatonic Scale

Another common scale used in rock improvisation is the *major pentatonic scale*. It is derived from the major scale and is usually used for songs in major keys. The major pentatonic scale has a brighter sound than the minor pentatonic, and is frequently used in country and southern rock styles. It is also often used in conjunction with minor pentatonic scales in blues-based tunes and as a more chord-specific scale; in other words, it may be applied to only certain chords in a progression.

The scale degrees used in the major pentatonic scale are:

1 2 3 5 6

For instance, the C Major Pentatonic scale is derived from the C Major scale as follows:

C Major Scale	1 C	2 D	3 E	4 F	5 G	6 A	7 B	1 C
C Major Pentatonic	1 C	2 D	3 E		5 G	6 A		

RELATIVE PENTATONIC SCALES

Example 119 below illustrates that the C Major Pentatonic and A Minor Pentatonic scales contain the same notes. This is an example of a *relative minor* relationship, as was first discussed on page 22 of this book. If you start and end the minor pentatonic scale on the ♭3 (in the A Minor Pentatonic scale, ♭3 is a C), you are playing the relative major pentatonic scale.

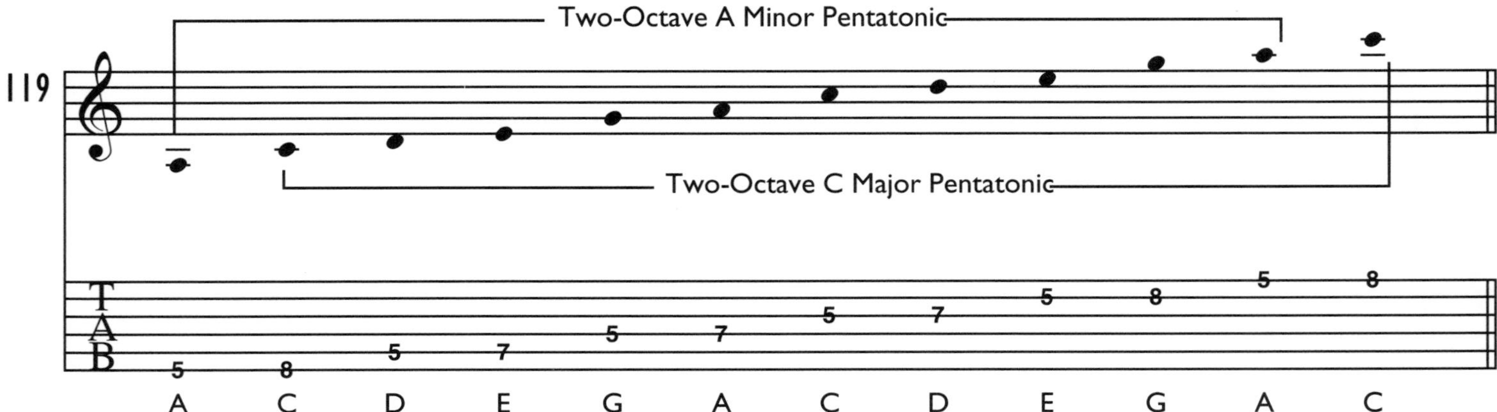

If you play Fingering #1 of the A Minor Pentatonic scale over an A Minor chord, you can easily hear the minor quality of the scale. Try playing the same notes over a C Major chord and you will hear how the same set of notes can function as a C Major Pentatonic scale. The difference between the A Minor and C Major Pentatonic scales lies in the way the player phrases their solo against the chords. For instance, over a C Major chord, resolving to the root (C) or the 3rd (E) will make the scale sound major. Over an A Minor chord, resolving to the root (A) or the ♭3 (C) will make the scale sound minor.

Notice that Fingering #1 of the major pentatonic scale is the same as Fingering #1 of the minor pentatonic scale (see page 33), but the roots are different.

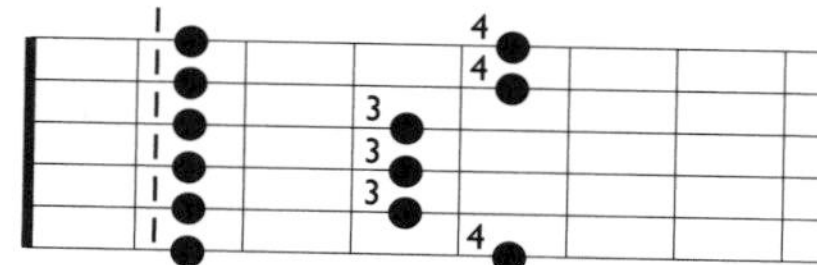

Try playing this scale starting on the 5th fret over the following chord progressions, and notice how it sounds minor over the one in A Minor, and major over the one in C Major.

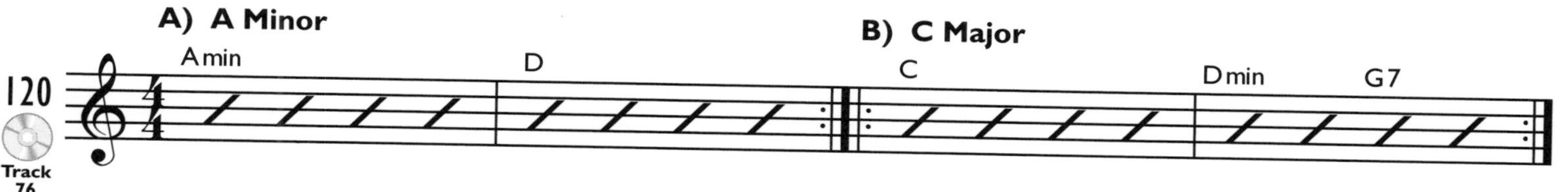

With practice, the similarities and differences will become apparent.

Remember that the minor pentatonic scale has a ♭3, and the major pentatonic scale has a ♮3. This is the most important difference between the two scales.

THE FIVE MAJOR PENTATONIC FINGERINGS

Just as there are five minor pentatonic fingerings, there are five fingerings for the major pentatonic scale.

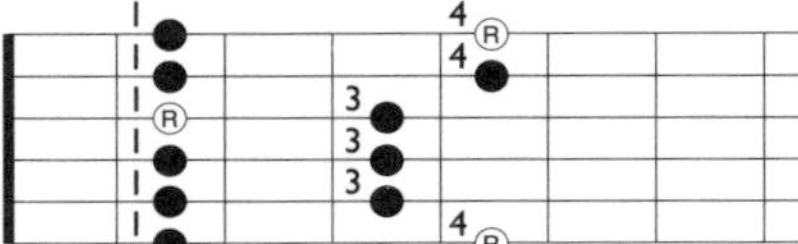

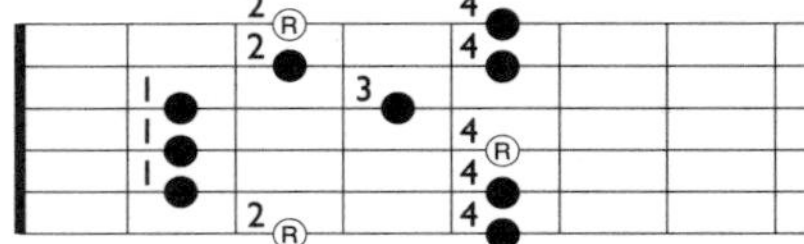

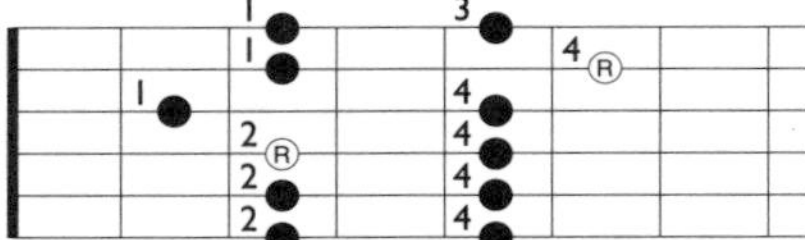

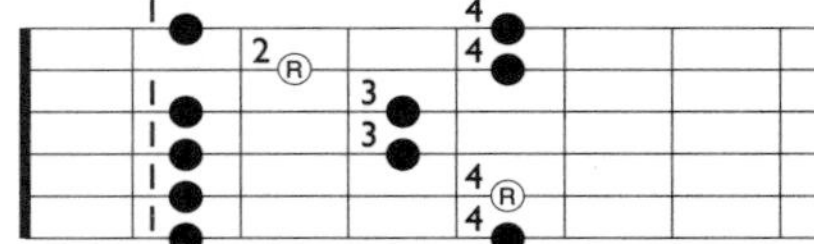

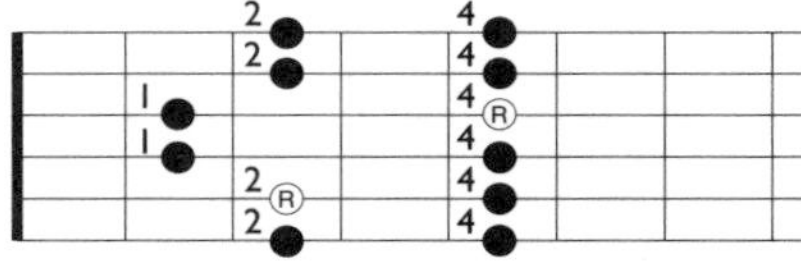

PHOTO • BOB LEAFE\STAR FILE, INC.

Kim Thayil of Soundgarden

SLIDING E MAJOR PENTATONIC

The concept of the sliding pentatonic scale, as introduced on page 31, works for the major pentatonic scale, too. Here it is for the E Major Pentatonic scale (E - F♯ - G♯ - B - C♯). Use it to play E Major Pentatonic across the entire fingerboard.

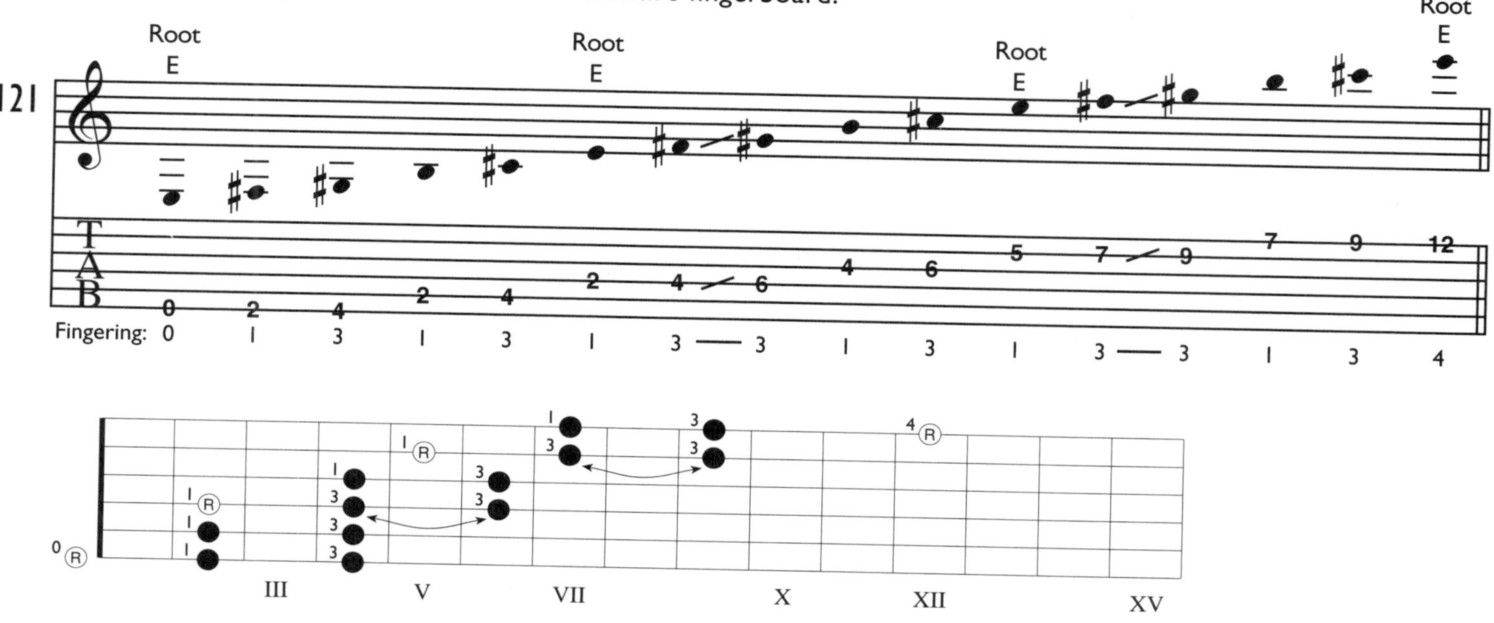

Use the sliding E Major Pentatonic scale to improvise over this chord progression.

Try using the E Major Pentatonic scale over the I chord (E) of this blues progression, but use the E Minor Pentatonic scale over IV (A) and V (B7).

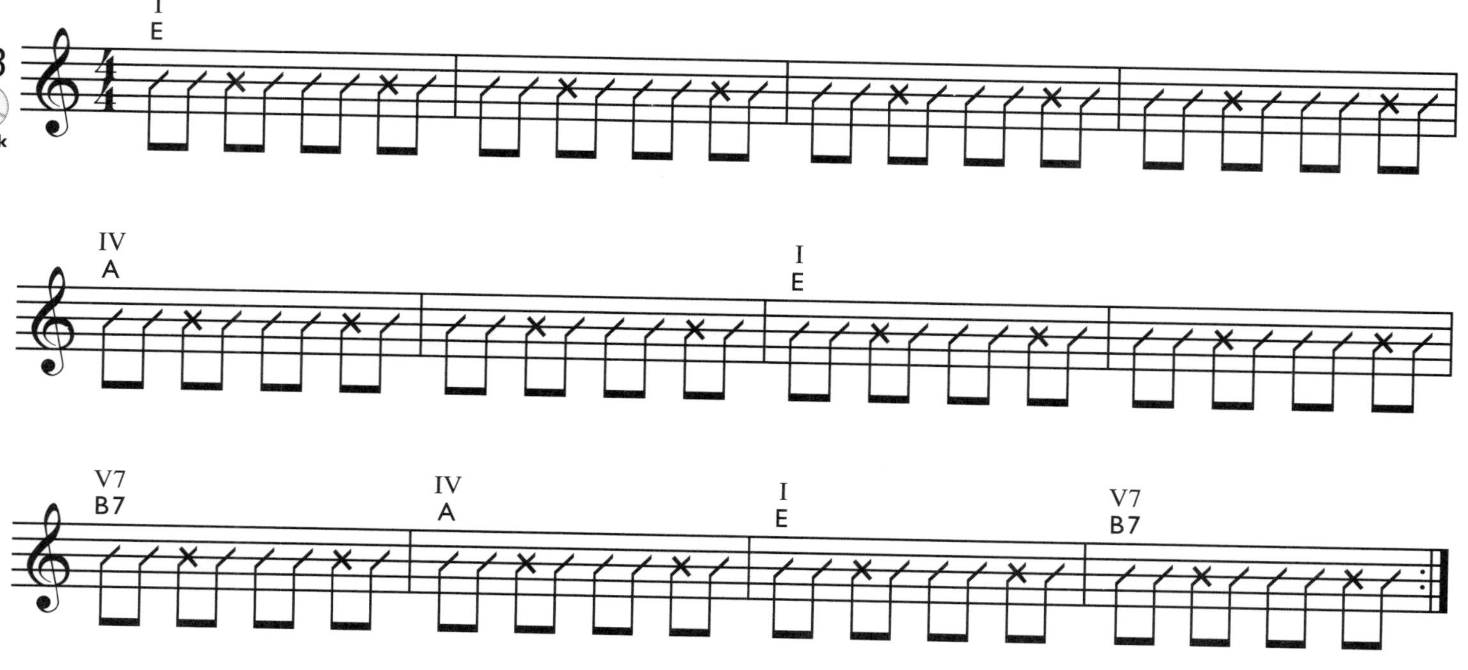

MAJOR PENTATONIC CONNECTIONS

As you observed in your study of the sliding E Major Pentatonic scale on page 87, we need to learn connecting routes between all the major pentatonic fingerings. Here are some sample connections in A to get you started. The brackets in the standard notation show which fingerings are being connected.

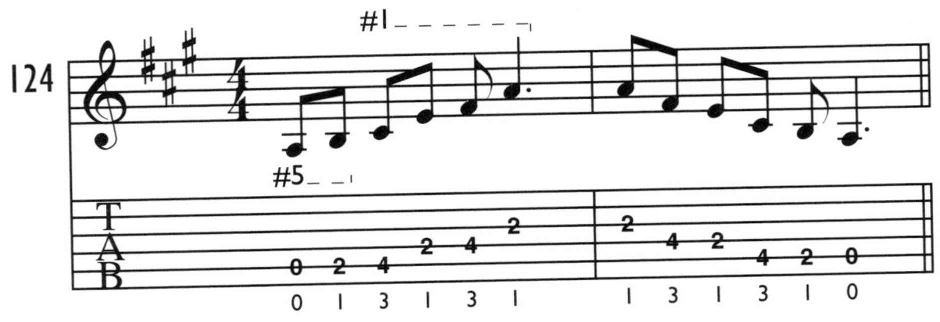

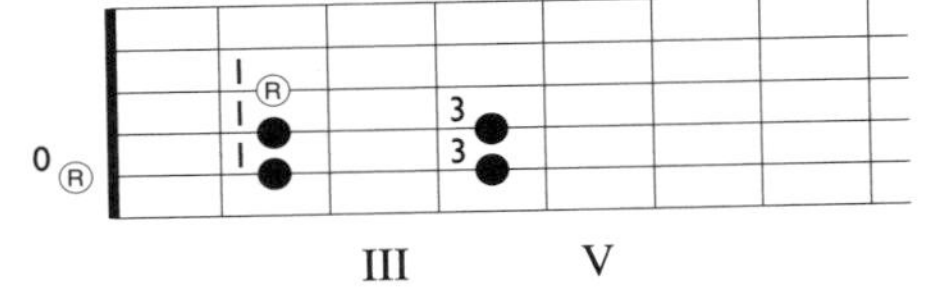

#5 _ _ _ _ ˌ = Notes with this bracket are from Fingering #5

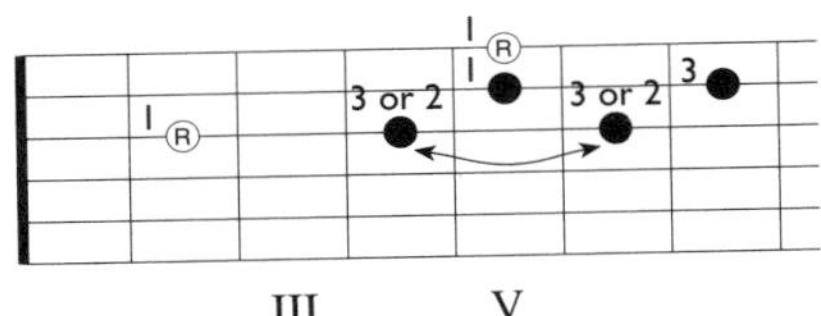

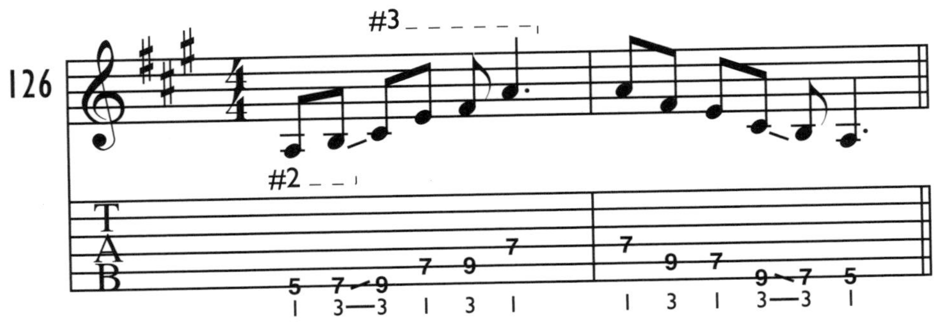

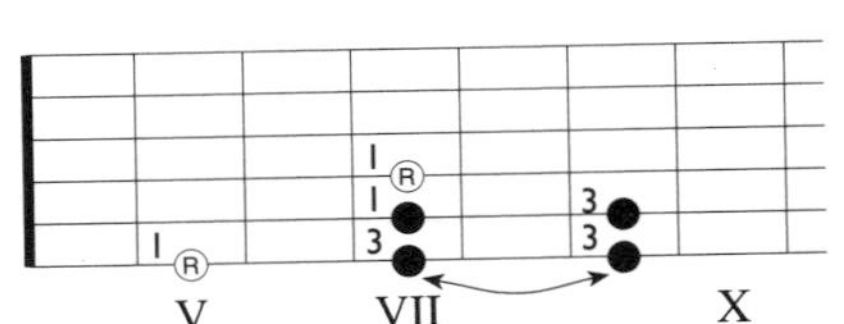

127
#4
#3
10 11 9 11 10 9 11 9 7
7 9 11 9 11 10
1 3—3 1 3 2
2 3 1 3—3 1

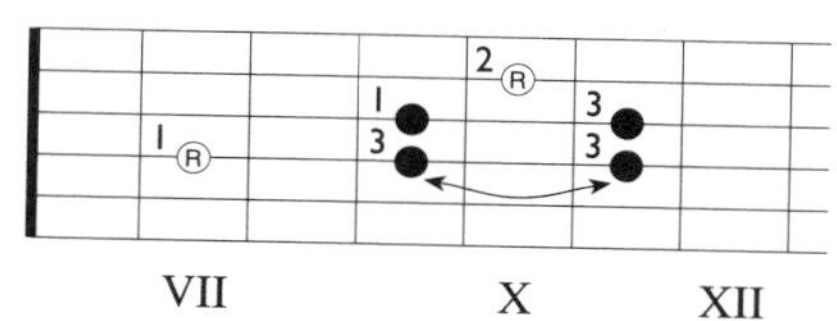
VII
X
XII

128
#1
#5
12 14 16 14 16 14
14 16 14 16 14 12
1 3—3 1 3 1
1 3 1 3—3 1

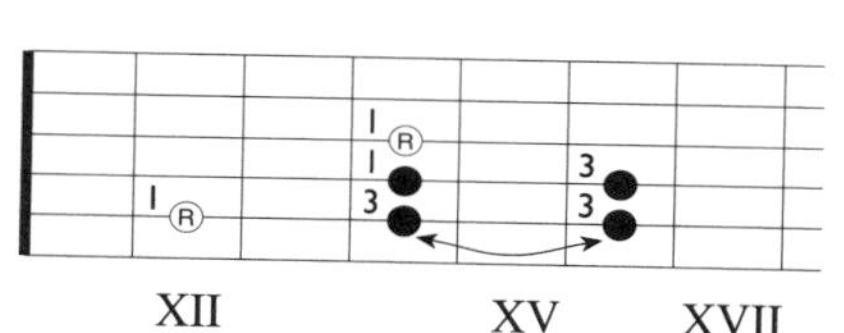
XII
XV
XVII

8va
129
#5
#4
10 12 14 12 14 17
17 14 12 14 12 10
1 3—3 1 3 4
4 3 1 3—3 1

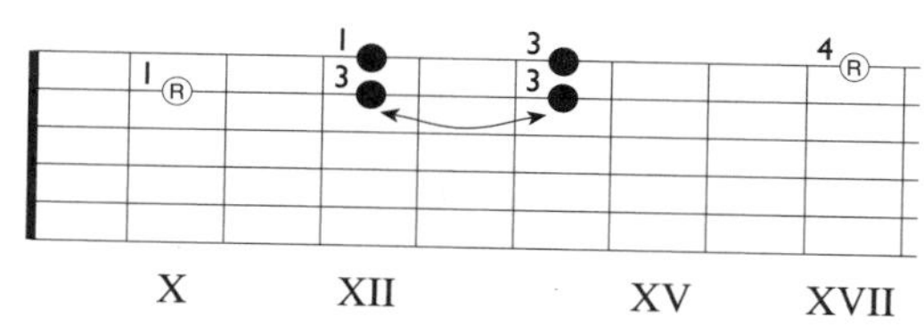
X
XII
XV
XVII

MAJOR PENTATONIC LICKS

Enjoy learning these major pentatonic licks, and try putting them to use in your solos. Then create some licks of your own.

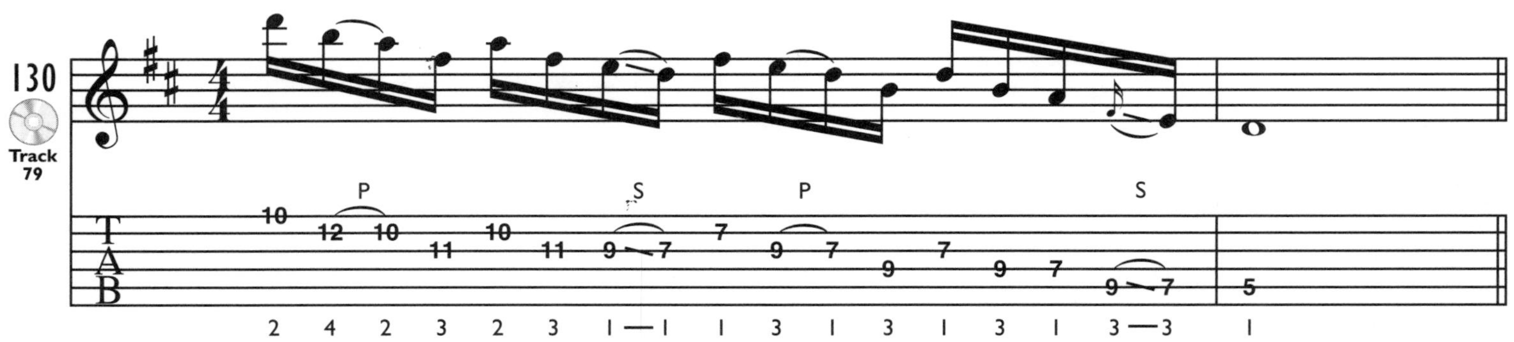

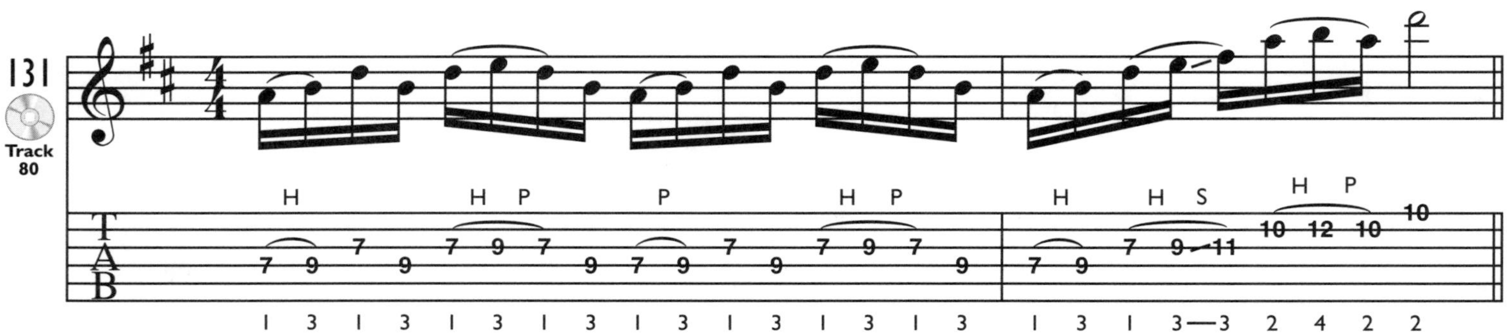

Swing the eighths in Example 132.

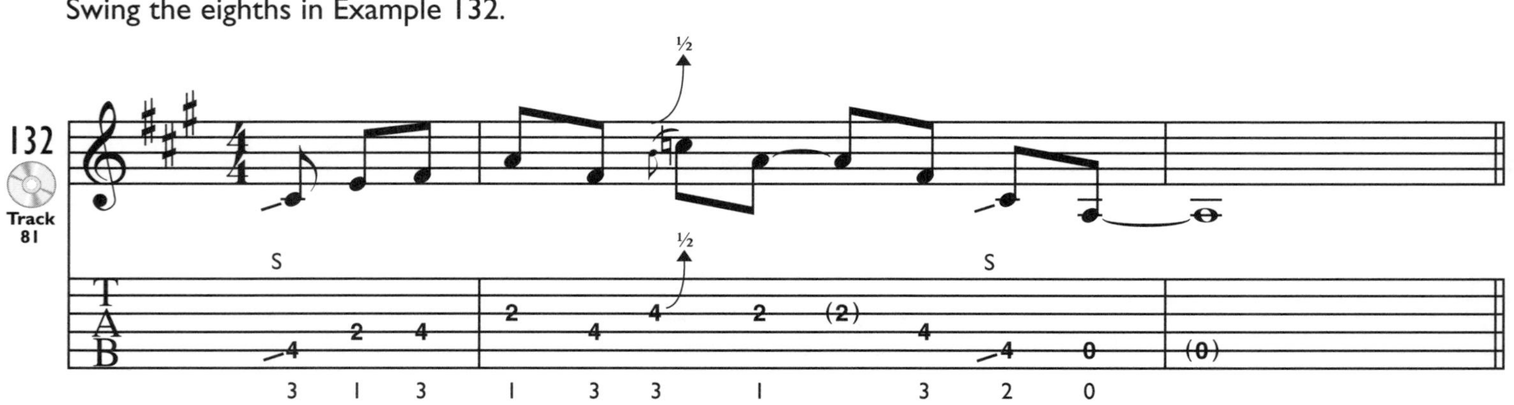

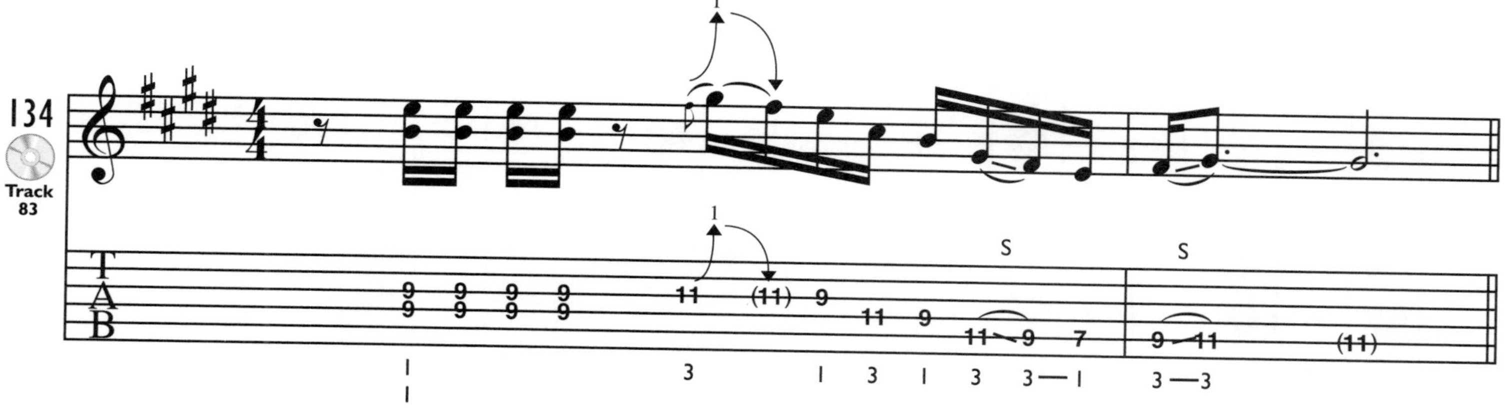

Steve Morse

PHOTO • GLEN LA FERMAN/COURTESY OF MCA

THE ENTIRE MAJOR PENTATONIC SYSTEM

THE FORMULA

1 2 3 5 6

The following diagram shows all the major-pentatonic fingerings in the key of A, starting at the 2nd fret. In this key, it is easy to see how the fingerings connect over most of the fingerboard.

THE FINGERINGS IN THE KEY OF A

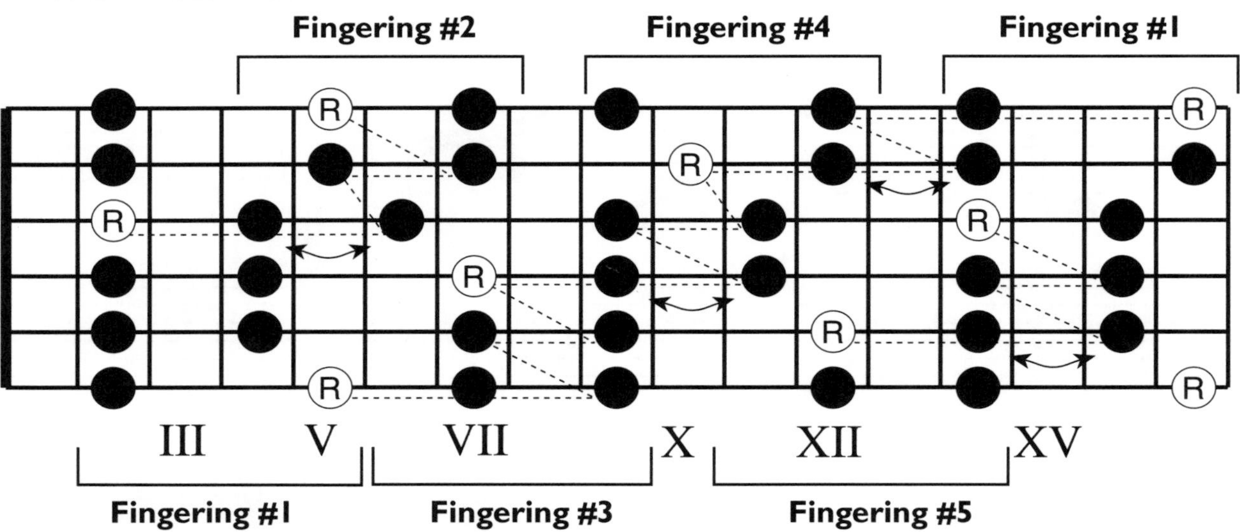

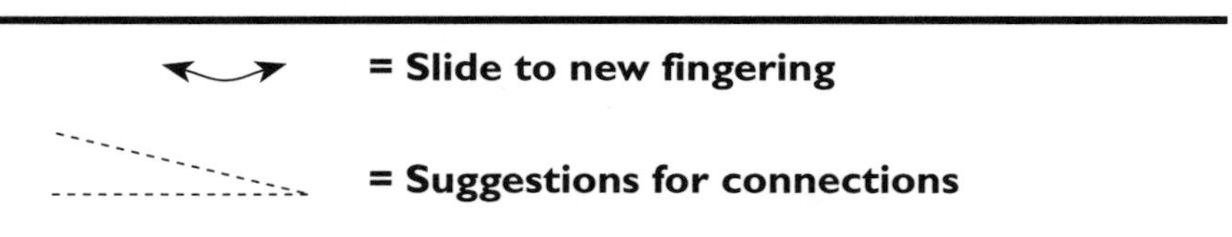

Congratulations! You have completed *Beginning Rock Guitar*. It's time to take a step up to the next level and continue your study in *Intermediate Rock Guitar*.

APPENDIX A

Suggested Songs for Practice

CHAPTER 3—POWER CHORDS

1. Iron Man - Black Sabbath
2. Any early Kinks
3. Master of Puppets - Metallica
4. Back in Black - AC/DC
5. Aqualung - Jethro Tull
6. Basket Case - GreenDay

CHAPTER 4—THE MINOR PENTATONIC SCALE

1. Any early Led Zeppelin
2. Any blues song
3. Purple Haze - Jimi Hendrix
4. Hey Joe - Jimi Hendrix
5. Sunshine of Your Love - Cream (Eric Clapton)
6. Alive - Pearl Jam

CHAPTER 5—LEFT-HAND TECHNIQUES

1. Rock & Roll - Led Zeppelin
2. Paranoid - Black Sabbath
3. I Know A Little - Lynyrd Skynyrd
4. Crazy Train - Ozzy Osbourne
5. Winona - Primus

CHAPTER 6—CHORDS AND RHYTHM GUITAR

1. White Room - Cream (Eric Clapton)
2. Any AC/DC
3. Stairway to Heaven - Led Zeppelin
4. Any Creedence Clearwater Revival
5. One - Metallica
6. Sample in a Jar - Phish

   for movable chords...

7. Johnny B. Goode - Chuck Berry
8. Rock & Roll Hootchie Koo - Johnny Winter, Rick Derringer
9. Roxanne - Police
10. Sultans of Swing - Dire Straits
11. Funk #49 - James Gang
12. Lightning Crashes - Live

CHAPTER 7 - MORE MINOR PENTATONICS

1. One Way Out - Allman Brothers
2. Any Eric Clapton
3. Mississippi Queen - Mountain (Leslie West)
4. Any Guns N' Roses
5. Enter Sandman - Metallica
6. Native Dance - Steve Morse
7. Are You Gonna Go My Way - Lenny Kravitz
8. Luminous Flesh Giants - Joe Satriani

CHAPTER 8—THE BLUES

1. Voodoo Chile - Jimi Hendrix
2. Any B. B. King
3. Any of John Mayall's Bluesbreakers with Eric Clapton
4. Any Stevie Ray Vaughn
5. T-Bone Shuffle - T-Bone Walker
6. Any Robert Cray
7. Still Alive and Well - Jeff Healy

CHAPTER 9—THE MAJOR PENTATONIC SCALE

1. Jessica - Allman Brothers
2. Drive My Car - Beatles
3. Hideaway - Eric Clapton with The Bluesbreakers
4. Any other Dickie Betts with The Allman Brothers
5. Keep on Growin' - Derek and the Dominoes (Eric Clapton)
6. River of Deceit - Mad Seasons

APPENDIX B

ROCK 'N ROLL BEGINNINGS
Chuck Berry
James Burton
Bo Diddley
Scottie Moore
Carl Perkins

THE BLUES
Albert Collins
Buddy Guy
Elmore James
Robert Johnson
Albert King
B. B. King
Muddy Waters

60s ROCK
Jeff Beck
Eric Clapton
George Harrison
Jimi Hendrix
Jimmy Page
Keith Richards

70s ROCK
Duane Allman
Larry Carlton
Steve Howe
Toni Iommi
Brian May
Joe Walsh

80s ROCK
Frank Gambale
Michael Hedges
Eric Johnson
Yngwie Malmsteen
Steve Morse
Randy Rhoads
Joe Satriani
Mike Stern
Steve Vai
Stevie Ray Vaughn
Eddie Van Halen
Zak Wylde

90s ROCK
Paul Gilbert
David Grissom
Warren Haynes
Lenny Kravitz
Mike McCready
Dave Navarro
John Petrucci
Blues Saraceno
Alex Skolnick
Kim Thayil

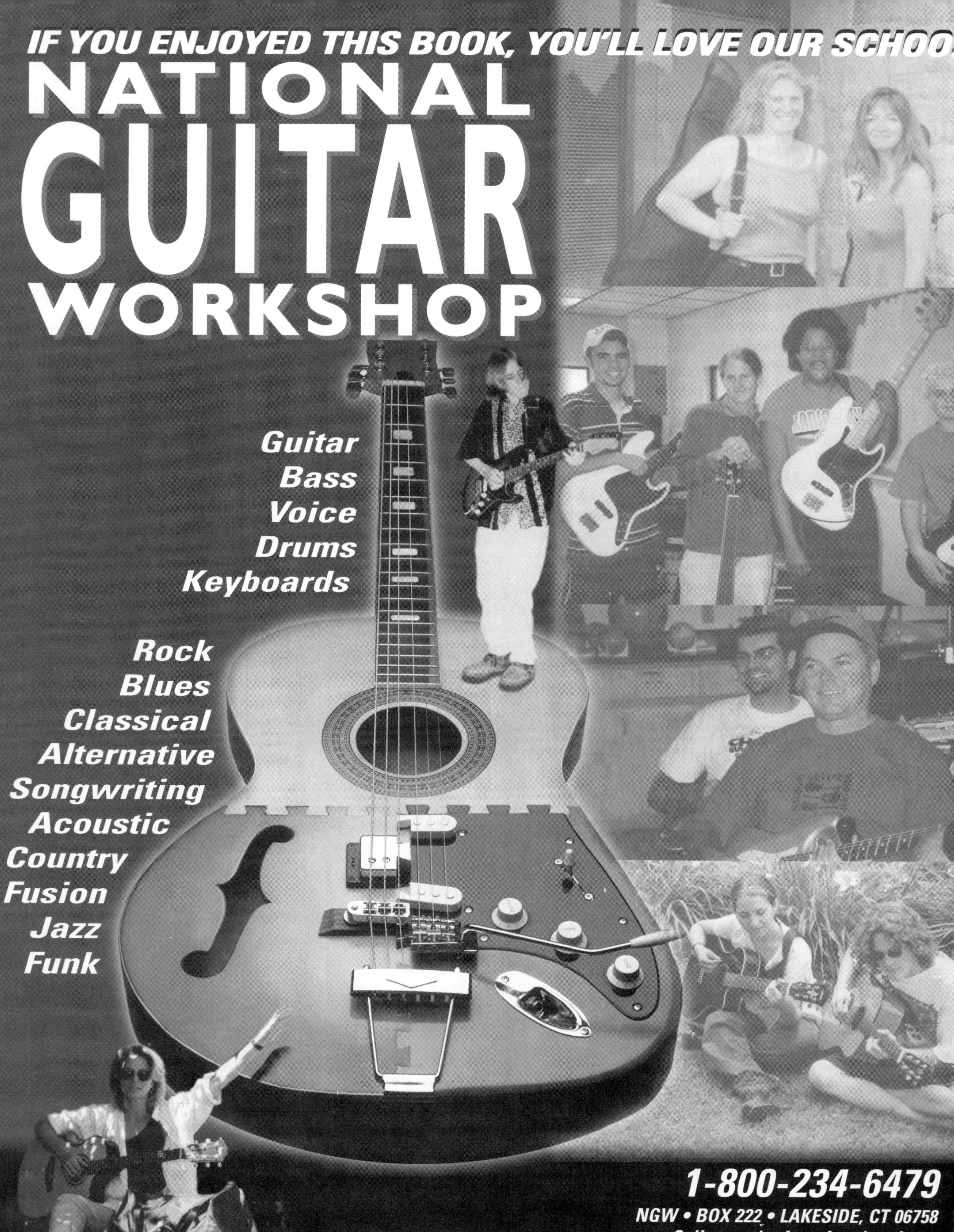

IF YOU ENJOYED THIS BOOK, YOU'LL LOVE OUR SCHOO
NATIONAL
GUITAR
WORKSHOP
Guitar
Bass
Voice
Drums
Keyboards
Rock
Blues
Classical
Alternative
Songwriting
Acoustic
Country
Fusion
Jazz
Funk
1-800-234-6479
NGW • BOX 222 • LAKESIDE, CT 06758
Call or write for a free brochure.